Dynamic PHOTOSHOP

M&T BOOKS

DANIEL GIORDAN

M&T Books
A Division of MIS:Press, Inc.
A Subsidiary of Henry Holt and Company, Inc.
115 West 18th Street
New York, New York 10011
http://www.mispress.com

Limits of Liability and Disclaimer of Warranty

First Edition—1997

Giordan, Daniel.
    Dynamic Photoshop / by Daniel Giordan.
        p. cm.
    ISBN 1-55851-562-3
    1. Computer Graphics. 2. Adobe Photoshop (Computer file) I. Title.
T385.G546 1997
006.6'869--dc21   97-20776
                                                                                  CIP

10 9 8 7 6 5 4 3 2 1

Design by Pronto Design & Production, Inc.

Associate Publisher: *Paul Farrell*

Managing Editor: *Shari Chappell*   **Production Editor:** *Maya Riddick*
Editor: *Rebekah Young*   **Technical Editor:** *Jonathan Lipkin*
Copy Edit Manager: *Karen Tongish*   **Copy Editor:** *Bert Shankle*

This book is dedicated to

my son Joshua…

Your timing is perfect, kid.

ACKNOWLEDGMENTS

Photoshop is my great digital love, and creating this book has been a real joy for me. I would like to thank those who helped me bring this project to fruition, as any author can tell you that a book like this is not a one man show; rather it is a team effort.

Thanks go to Rebekah Young, editor at MIS:Press, who helped shape the content and direction of this book. I especially appreciate that she gave me free reign to express what I felt was important, while at the same time serving as a great sounding board and reality check. Thanks also to Kurt Andrews, Production Director at Henry Holt, Inc., and Maya Riddick the Senior Production Editor at MIS:Press who shepherded this book from manuscript into printed form. The entire team at MIS:Press did a great job with this, and I truly enjoyed working with them.

In addition, I appreciate the work of Jonathan Lipkin, the technical editor. He was a tremendous help in dotting the i's and crossing the t's, making sure that the material presented here is 100% accurate.

Thanks also go to Brian Gill at Studio B Productions. Thanks for your tenacious persistence in making this project happen, Brian. You really played an important role.

Finally, thanks must go to my family, who patiently allow me to go into authorial hibernation each time a project or deadline looms on the horizon. My wife Barbara has been incredibly patient and supportive, as she is with all my endeavors. It just would not be possible for me to do what I do were it not for her encouragement and belief.

As I write this Barbara is two days past her due date, waiting to deliver my first child, whom the doctors tell us is a boy. Her due date was April 4, and my final date for this manuscript was April 8th. I appreciate her willingness to do whatever it takes for a deadline ;). I really should thank my son Joshua, who is already scoring points with his old man by sitting tight until this book finished. Snug and secure in his warm little home, he definitely had the better end of the deal. Alright boy, the project's over, you can come out now… and hurry it up, 'cause I can't wait to see your face.

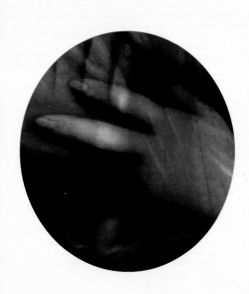

Contents

INTRODUCTION

The goal of this book is to empower the artist to work creatively with Adobe Photoshop. To that end, it examines how to work intuitively, combining pixels and images in the design process. Scattered throughout the book are step-by-step exercises I've called Recipes. The recipes are placed so that the points covered will relate to the context of the surrounding text. They allow you to practice the main concepts being discussed at that point.

The first section, composed of Chapters 1-4, looks at how to implement an intuitive design workflow. A well-considered workflow not only gets things done faster, but in many cases, it actually improves the finished product. Because Photoshop offers such a tremendous array of design options, it is important to understand how to flow from one option to another. We will examine the main areas in Photoshop that need to be mastered, so that we can apply the full breadth of its resources at any time. We will also learn how to optimize tools, applications, and our computer systems, in order to become more responsive and creative.

The second section, comprised of Chapters 5 and 6, looks at how to combine pixels in achieving various digital effects. The use of Blending Modes and filters creates many of the signature digital effects we are all used to seeing. They also hold forth a wide array of options that are less recognizable as a finished product, but just as important to the creative process. These chapters lay out the parameters of what filters and Blending Modes can achieve.

The final section, Chapters 7 and 8, looks specifically at how to composite multiple images into a single design. This process goes far beyond menu options and mouse clicks. In light of this, the fundamental issues of perspective, focus, and color are examined, with a specific focus on how they impact a digital composite. Chapter 8 also gives specific advice on spotting, creating shadows, and morphing two objects together.

part

1

INTUITIVE WORKFLOW

Chapter 1

WORKING SMART:
Speed and Safety

Many people we consider to be highly creative are actually just able to work very efficiently, creating more design possibilities.

Much of the creative process is trial and error. Try something and see what happens. Does it work? If not, try something else. Does that work? To work intuitively, we need constant feedback on how design choices impact the final product. Should I apply a filter here? How about adjusting the curves. You hang on to the things that work and you discard what doesn't. This chapter will look at how you can work though a variety of design choices faster and more efficiently.

Each creative decision allows you to gather more data, which results in designs that have more depth and richness. As you work along, then, you are building on each decision, creating a stronger end-product. Many people we consider to be highly creative are actually just able to work very efficiently, creating more design possibilities.

To generate more material, you need a machine that can keep pace with the creative process. Each action generates several new options and if you don't act immediately, they're often lost. Therefore, you need to work quickly in order to hang on to the ideas that come and go as you're creating. That means you need to have a machine that doesn't make you wait forever between actions.

The second component in making effective design choices is having a process that lets you move fluidly between varying results, choosing what works best for each situation. This process should allow you to undo something that doesn't work, jump back three steps to a previous version, and hop two steps sideways to another option that you considered in the beginning. As you're able to evaluate and move between versions of your work, you will find yourself taking more risks. As you take more risks, you will collect a more diverse set of data, which will make your designs more effective.

The Need for Speed

Although we have come a very long way in making our machines go faster, they still don't seem to be able to keep up with our hands, eyes, and ideas. The chief areas to focus on in hardware optimization are the processor and RAM. Advances in storage technology also have made the hard drive a contributing factor to system speed. Video cards and processor accelerators round out the list of hardware tweaks you can make, if you have the energy and the cash.

The Processor

If you are going to play in the imaging arena, you need a system with a fast processor. Processors are rated for their speed in megahertz, which refers to the number of calculations the processor can make in any given time span. Think of it as the speed of a car as it travels on the highway. You want a processor that safely allows your data to travel on the Autobahn, rather than restricted to a 55 mph speed limit.

At this writing, the speed of processors has pushed past the 300 MHz barrier, with no end in sight. Silicon is being developed now that may double these rates in as little as 12 to 18 months. The PowerPC 60x chip and the Pentium processor both deliver blinding speed and will continue to evolve into faster systems. While it's not necessary to have the absolute fastest machine at all times, make sure you have at least a Power Mac or a Pentium system. Don't even pretend that you can do imaging with less.

Computer magazines and catalogs abound with processor upgrade options that promise to turn your old has-been computer into a speed demon. But remember that a processor upgrade may not give you additional expansion, a wider data path, or more RAM slots. Considering the way prices on brand new CPUs have been plummeting, the case for a processor upgrade is not as compelling as it once was.

Memory

RAM plays a critical role in the overall health of your system. While you should purchase as fast a processor as possible, you should not max out your budget without leaving room to buy memory. It's kind of like buying a house. Imagine that your goal is to live in a comfortable house. You could spend all of your money on a mansion, but you won't be very happy if you have nothing left to spend on furniture. Sitting on a cold mansion floor is not very comfortable.

People do something similar when they spend all of their money on a CPU without leaving anything for RAM. You should have absolutely no less than 32 MB of RAM to run Photoshop, and this is a concession. In reality, 64 MB is more desirable if you are working with files of any reasonable size. As we get into allocating RAM for Photoshop and how RAM works, you will understand how important this is. You could in fact argue that RAM is the single most important factor in a system, although it goes hand-in-hand with the processor itself.

WHAT IS RAM?

Plenty of books cover this subject, so I will be brief. RAM is a place where data is stored so that the processor can access it and make its calculations. All by itself, the data sitting on your hard drive is not able to get moving fast enough to smoothly plug into the speeds of the processor. It takes so much time for the data to be pulled off the hard drive and plugged into the system that the processor can sit idle much of the time. If all we had were processors and hard drives, then computers would be pretty worthless. RAM dramatically decreases the time it takes to send data through the processor. It's kind of like a relay race where the data is the baton, and the drive, RAM, and processor are the runners. They each take off with the data as fast as they can, smoothly passing it off to each other to complete the race as quickly as possible. When data is loaded into RAM it becomes much more fluid

and active. It is able to respond to the processor when it makes a request at 300 MHz, and information gets processed. Information processing is a matter of frequency and synchronized speed.

ALLOCATING RAM IN PHOTOSHOP

Remember that RAM is a communal space, shared by the System file, extensions, control panels, and a host of invisible files and scripts that are running behind the scenes at all times. Photoshop is fighting with all these other components for memory space as it is loaded. If it has too little, systems crash, slow down, or just don't work the way they should.

This is why you need to allocate as much RAM as possible to Photoshop before you launch the program. This stakes Photoshop's claim to the available RAM, and ensures that it will have enough to work with. You should allocate 3 to 5 times the size of your largest file as RAM for Photoshop.

This allows room for the application itself and ensures that things will run smoothly while designing. Nothing throws a wrench into fluid workflow like a system crash or a sluggish machine.

Storage and Speed

In addition to upgrading the RAM and processor, the hard drive can play a major role in optimizing Photoshop. A faster hard drive will allow applications and files to open faster and will speed up file copying, deleting, and other disk-intensive actions. For Photoshop users, the hard drive is even more important because of the role played by the scratch disk. (See "Setting Scratch Disks" in the optimization checklist, later in this chapter). As an invisible partition of the hard drive, the scratch disk is constantly creating drive activity as data is stored and retrieved. An upgrade here will dramatically improve Photoshop's performance.

A Fast/Wide hard drive has a wider data path than a conventional SCSI drive. It is approximately twice the speed of any drive hanging off the native or standard SCSI port. The wider data path uses a special connector that requires the installation of a PCI expansion card. Fast/Wide drives cost only a few hundred dollars more than conventional drives, and the results are impressive for anyone using large files or a large volume of files.

Once you have a Fast/Wide drive, it's easy to move up a level to a Fast/Wide striped array (also called RAID 0). A striped array consists of two Fast/Wide drives connected through one or two Fast/Wide PCI controller cards via software. The striped disk array splits the data in two and writes it simultaneously to both drives. The transfer rates are phenomenal, and once you've used a disk array you'll never want to go back to your standard hard drive.

The average *sustained* transfer rates for a standard internal or external hard drive are around 4 MB per second. Moving to Fast/Wide ups that number to around 7 MB per second, and a disk array can up the transfer to well over 15 to 20 MB per second. A faster technology called Ultra SCSI pushes these rates even further, to something closer to 30 MB per second. Keep an eye on this technology and get the fastest hard drive you can afford.

A fast video card that supports a high resolution is also an important piece of the puzzle. If you are running off your system's on-board video, make sure that you have enough VRAM to support a large monitor at the highest resolution possible. Another upgrade to consider is a RAM cache, a RAM module set aside for instruction sets frequently used by the processor. Cache RAM can deliver these frequently used instructions even faster than standard RAM. Cache RAM can be installed in 256KB or 1024KB.

You can see a 30% to 50% performance gain by installing a cache card in your machine, which makes it an option worth considering.

Optimization Checklist

What follows is an eight-point checklist to optimize a system for Photoshop. It covers memory, color calibration, preference settings, and various other tweaks that all add up to a more intuitive and responsive machine.

1. *Allocating memory.* When allocating RAM for Photoshop you should calculate 3 to 5 times the size of your average Photoshop file. That means that a 10 MB file would require 30 to 50 MB of RAM. If you don't have that much, then give Photoshop all you've got, reserving 5 to 10 MB for the system. To allocate memory:

   • Highlight the Photoshop application icon and choose **Get Info** from the File menu (**Command/Control-I**).

• In the Get Info box, type in the minimum and preferred memory sizes, based on the guidelines discussed earlier, and the amount of memory you have installed in your machine (Figure 1.1). Click **OK** to exit.

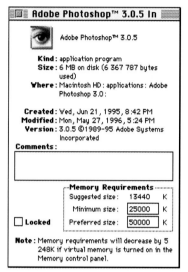

Figure 1.1 *Allocate memory to Photoshop through the Get Info box.*

The suggestions for decreasing memory size by employing Virtual Memory do not work as well with Photoshop as they do with other applications. Try to stay away from enabling Virtual Memory with Photoshop, as the gains are virtually nil and problems can result. As mentioned earlier, buy more RAM.

2. *Setting scratch disks.* A scratch disk is a place to store the pattern, snapshot, and undo information used by Photoshop, as an alternative to using RAM space. Working behind the scenes, Photoshop stores this information on a portion of your hard drive and accesses it as needed. If you have more than one drive, you can designate which drive Photoshop uses for the scratch disk. Keep in mind that the faster the drive, the more responsive Photoshop will be to

revert commands, pattern fills, and the like. You should also keep in mind that if you fill up the scratch disk, you will not be allowed to save your file. Keep an eye on your scratch disk and make sure it has several hundred megabytes in available space. If you have more than one drive, you can set your scratch disk as follows:

• Select **Plug-ins & Scratch Disks** under the Preferences command in the File menu.

• Click and hold on the **Primary** pop-up menu and select the desired drive. You may also designate a second disk, which acts as a back-up if the primary disk is full (Figure 1.2). Click **OK** to exit.

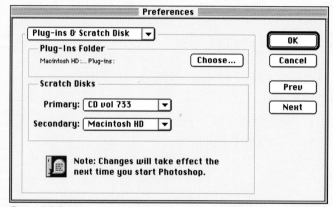

Figure 1.2 *Set the target scratch disk in the Photoshop Plug-ins & scratch disks preferences box.*

3. *Saving file shortcuts.* If you don't need the preview icons created by Photoshop when a file is saved, you can disable them. This will speed up Photoshop each time a file is saved. In addition, as version 2.5 dims in our collective memory, it is more likely that you can disable the Photoshop 2.5 compatibility option. This option saves a flattened version of the file along with the layered one in case you need to use version 2.5 to edit it. To disable these options:

• Select **Saving Files** from the Preferences command in the File menu.

- In the Image Previews pop-up menu, select **Never Save**.

- In the Options section of the window, uncheck the **2.5 Compatibility** box and click **OK** to exit.

4. *Export clipboard.* By default, Photoshop tries to export whatever is in its own clipboard to the system's clipboard each time you close the application. This is usually a waste of time because the formats are generally not compatible with other applications. Disabling this feature is almost always a good idea. To shut off the Export Clipboard feature:

- Select **General** from the Preferences command in the File menu.

- Uncheck **Export Clipboard** in the Options section, and click **OK** to exit (Figure 1.3).

Figure 1.3 Deselecting **Export Clipboard** *will help Photoshop to close files more quickly, without trying to save the clipboard contents.*

5. *Monitor positioning.* The physical positioning of the monitor itself is often overlooked in optimizing a system. Be sure to avoid direct or intense light, as well as glare on the screen. Fluorescents are deadly to the appearance of images on screen and should be avoided if possible.

Once the monitor is in a good position, adjust the monitor's external brightness and contrast controls until the screen looks clear and balanced. Once the controls are set, tape over them or mark them to ensure that they are not accidentally changed.

6. *Setting the monitor's gamma.* Gamma affects the overall brightness and tonal range of your display. You can calibrate the gamma using the Gamma control panel that ships with Photoshop. The Gamma control panel allows you to modify the contrast of your display, as well as the color balance. Because so many other color modifications are used in your system, it is advisable to adjust the overall contrast and leave the color calibration to ColorSync or the Monitor preferences in Photoshop (more on this shortly). If it is not already loaded on your machine (it will be in the Control Panels folder), you will find it under **Adobe Photoshop: Goodies: Calibration: Separation Sources**. Add the Gamma control panel to your control panels folder and restart your machine. To calibrate your monitor's gamma:

- Open the Gamma control panel.

- Make sure the On button in the lower-left corner is selected.

- Set the Target Gamma. In most cases, 1.8 is representative of the tonal range for imaging on the Macintosh, and 2.5 is standard for the PC.

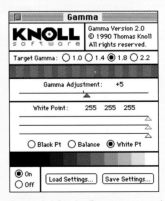

Figure 1.4 Set the Gamma target at 1.8, and adjust the Gamma Adjustment triangle until the bands are a uniform gray.

- Move the Gamma Adjustment triangle until the gray bands above it appear to merge with each other, creating one solid band of color (Figure 1.4). Close the control panel for the changes to take effect.

7. *Monitor setup.* Configure the Monitor setup controls in Photoshop to make color rendition more accurate. Photoshop uses your specific monitor's ColorSync profiles to calibrate the color, so make sure the control panel profiles are loaded and available. To change the Monitor setup:

   - Choose **Monitor Set-up** from the Color Controls command in the File menu.

   - Click on the **Monitors** pop-up menu in the Monitor Parameters section, and select the closest match for your display. This will automatically set the remaining options in this section.

   - Select the appropriate lighting conditions from the Ambient Light pop-up menu in the Room Parameters section, and click **OK** to exit.

   *If your monitor type is not an available option in the Monitors pop-up menu, select **Default**. Choose **6500** as a White Point, and select the Phosphors accordingly, depending on the type monitor you own.*

8. *Group palettes according to the way you work.* By default, the palettes in Photoshop are grouped together based on Adobe's assumption of how they will be used. You can regroup them to your liking by dragging them from one open palette window to another. You should consider which palette combinations get most of your attention and customize them accordingly.

Putting the Flow in Workflow

Getting the CPU to go faster is just one aspect of creating a smooth workflow. More important to the process is being able to compare, contrast, and integrate different versions of your design. This will allow you to change directions if something isn't working, temper an effect, or integrate the best components of different versions.

The goal is to create a strategy that allows access to the various controls and options within Photoshop. This requires an understanding of how Photoshop works with images, knowing where clipboards and image buffers are kept, and how many different versions of these buffers can be accessed at any given time. Understanding where things are kept and how to get at them is critical to being able to move deftly through Photoshop without painting yourself into a corner.

First, you need a solid understanding of where Photoshop stores data as you are working on it and how it is accessed. Photoshop allows you to access data that has been saved to the clipboard from a number of tools and menu commands. In addition, it also gives a number of alternative clipboard-like spaces for additional image information to be stored. Understanding these options and how they differ is the first step in creating a solid workflow strategy.

Global Data Storage Options

There are three general areas to save data from your design: to another file, to the scratch disk, and to a layer. The term *data* is used rather than *file* or *version* because it is possible to save a portion of a file, such as a layer or a selection, to another place.

SAVING DATA TO ANOTHER FILE

There are many ways to save versions or portions of a file to another file. They are listed next to give a general overview of how this can be achieved.

- Select **Save a Copy** from the file menu, and then name and save the file. This lets you keep working on the same file while off-loading a separate version to another place.

- Select **Save As** from the file menu. This renames the current file along with all of its modifications, while reverting the original file to its last saved version.

- Make a selection, copy it, open a new file, and paste. The new file default dialog box always reflects the size of the current clipboard selection. Click **OK** without changing anything in the dialog box, and paste the image to the new file.

- Duplicate to a new file with **Image: Duplicate**. This is similar to the Save a Copy procedure.

- Duplicate a layer to a new file. This saves only the contents of the designated layer to a separate file. This procedure allows you to save certain aspects of an image, without saving everything. Select **Duplicate** from the Layer menu and enter the new file information.

The end result of these actions is a stand-alone file containing an image, layer, or selection. This approach can serve to keep a separate version of the file in case the original is lost. This allows freedom to modify the image with the ability to get back to the starting point at any time.

Saving data to another file is also a great alternative to saving image versions to layers within the same file. It can streamline the overall file size, and make things easier to manage. Unlike layers, which max out at a certain point, the number of alternative stand-alone files is limited only by the free disk space in your system.

The drawbacks to the new file approach are that the information in the new file feels removed from the original. When a layer is made, it stays with the original file at all times. You can turn it on or off, but it's always there. With so many new files floating around on your hard drive, unless you have a great naming scheme and storage system, keeping track of the various versions could be intimidating.

SAVING TO ALTERNATE AREAS

There are times when you want a portion of your image set off to one side for safekeeping. The Mac OS designers called this place a *clipboard*. Photoshop takes this idea a few steps further, using the clipboard as a starting point and offering numerous other places for keeping information. The other places are outlined next, and you should become familiar with them.

Revert The Revert command takes the entire image back to the last saved version, which of course, is stored on the scratch disk portion of the drive. It is activated by choosing the **Revert** command from the File menu. Be sure you have saved the file at least once, otherwise the command is grayed out and inaccessible.

Undo This one should need no introduction, at least to anyone using a Macintosh. (Windows users are now also using this handy command.) Undo takes you back one step. You access Undo in the same place as every other Macintosh program ever written: under the Edit menu.

Copy Copy is almost as familiar to us as Undo. Copy saves a version of an image or selection to the clipboard (housed in the scratch disk), which can be pasted back when necessary.

Snapshot The Snapshot command saves a current version of your file to the scratch disk. This feature is extremely useful, as we will see in the integration section that follows. To save a snapshot of a single layers contents, select **Take Snapshot** under the Edit menu. To take a snapshot of all of the layers in your entire image, select **Take Merged Snapshot** (Figure 1.5).

Figure 1.5 To save a snapshot of the current layer, select **Take Snapshot** from the Edit Menu.

Define Pattern Define Pattern saves a selected rectangle as a pattern to be repeated as a tiled image when it's reapplied. While this command can lead to some interesting graphic effects, it is also useful to those looking for other places to store images. If you select the entire image, you can save it as a pattern. If you apply the pattern to an area larger than the entire image, it tiles. But, because you will probably reapply it to the same area as before, it goes back in exactly the same way as a snapshot. To use Define Pattern to store data, choose **Select All** from the Select menu, and choose **Define Pattern** under the Edit menu. This will write a copy of the entire image to the scratch disk (Figure 1.6).

Figure 1.6 *With the entire image selected, selecting* **Define Pattern** *sends a full copy of the image to the scratch disk.*

REAPPLYING DATA FROM OTHER AREAS

At any given time, you can have five different versions of your image saved through the Revert, Snapshot, Define Pattern, Copy and Undo commands. As you are gathering information to these different areas, be sure not to save the image. Doing so will wipe out the contents of the Snapshot and Undo options. It is easy to do a save with a Revert command in mind, only to find that you've purged other information. Conversely, Version 4 added a Purge command in the Edit menu, which allows you to manually purge the contents of the areas we've been discussing. Given the overhead these areas exact in performance and space, this is an excellent addition.

Once you've gathered all the information, how do you reapply it to the image? Some options are obvious, others are subtle, but taken as a whole, they amount to a very secure net that supports your workflow.

The Undo option is obvious, selecting **Undo** takes you back to the next step. This is the most remedial of all of the Reapply options. Another obvious option is that selecting **Paste** will apply the contents of the clipboard as a separate layer. These global applications are very limiting compared to the other Apply options: the Fill command and the Rubber Stamp tool.

RECIPE: PIX IN PIX

Pix in Pix is an image treatment that was popularized by Kai Krause in the Kai's Powertip series, as well as in some of his lectures and online chats. It is an effect that serious Photoshop designers should know about. The basic approach is to create a grid made up of tiny cells of the original image (in our example, the globe). The grid is superimposed over the entire image, giving the sense that it is made up of smaller versions of the same image. Here's how it works:

1. After sharpening the image and increasing the contrast as much as possible, select the object that will serve as the cell in the final picture. The globe in this example was selected with the Paths tool, but you can arrive at your selection in any way that seems appropriate (Figure 1.7).

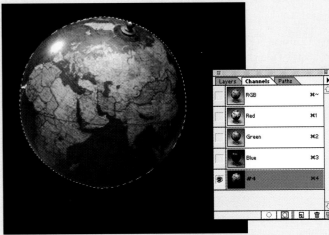

Figure 1.8 *Paste the selection into a new channel.*

Figure 1.7 *Select the object with the Paths tool.*

2. Copy the selection (**Command/Control-C**).

3. Activate the Channels palette (**Window: Show Channels**), and create a new channel by selecting **New Channel** from the Channels Palette Options pop-up menu.

4. Paste the copied selection into the new channel. It will come in as a grayscale image (Figure 1.8).

5. With the contents of the new channel still selected, select **Layers: Transform: Scale**. Holding down the **Shift** key to maintain the proportions of the image, select a corner handle and shrink the object down to the size for one of the actual cells. This size will vary depending on the object and the image. Click on the **Move** tool, and click the **Apply** button to apply the transformation (Figure 1.9).

6. Draw a marquee around the transformed image. Draw the marquee as close to the object as possible, taking care to maintain even spacing between the object and the marquee on all four sides. Select **Edit: Define Pattern** (Figure 1.10).

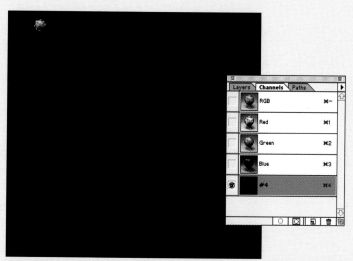

Figure 1.9 Scale the selection to the final cell size.

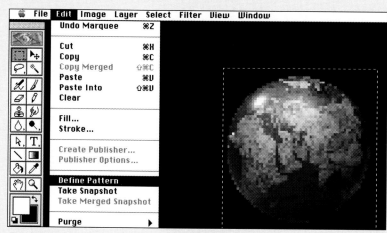

Figure 1.10 Select the image and choose **Define Pattern**.

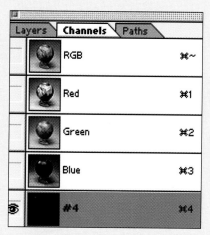

Figure 1.11 Fill the new channel with the repeating globe pattern.

7. Choose **Select All** from the Select menu. Choose **Fill** from the Edit menu, selecting **Pattern** from the Use pop-up menu, leaving the opacity at 100%, and the mode at normal. As a result, you will have a single channel filled with repeating tiles of your scaled-down image (Figure 1.11).

8. Activate the RGB composite channel and select **Load Selection** from the Select menu. Select **Channel #4** from the Source menu, check the **Invert** box, and click **OK** (Figure 1.12). You will now have a grid of selection lines over the entire image.

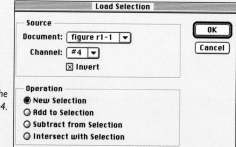

Figure 1.12 Load the selection from Channel #4.

14

RECIPE: CONTINUED

9. Click on the background color swatch and choose a dark neutral gray somewhere around the 75% tonal range. Press **Delete** to fill the selection with a neutral gray (Figure 1.13).

10. Select **Invert** from the Select menu and heighten the contrast on the area inside the globes. In this case, **Image: Adjust: Curves** was selected, the highlights were raised, and the shadows were lowered (Figure 1.14).

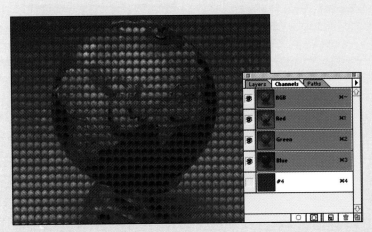

Figure 1.13 Delete the background to a dark gray.

Figure 1.15 The final image.

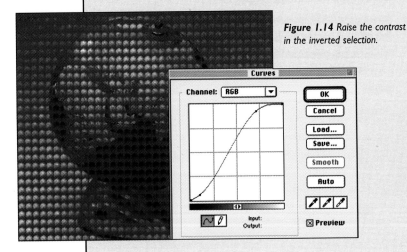

Figure 1.14 Raise the contrast in the inverted selection.

11. In addition to curves, you could also use brightness/contrast, levels, or any other tonal correction method. Let the image dictate which method is best (Figure 1.15).

The Fill command allows you to make any selection and fill it with the contents of the clipboard, snapshot, or pattern data. It also lets you fill with the foreground or background color, black and white, or gray. You can also vary the opacity of the fill. (A discussion of Preserve Transparency would necessitate the description of layers, transparent layers, and a special context in which that would be relevant. It comes later in the book.) To use the Fill command:

1. Select **Fill** from the Edit menu.
2. In the dialog box, click on the **Use** pop-up menu, selecting **Pattern**, **Saved**, or **Snapshot**. (The clipboard is not available through the Fill command.)
3. Set the Blending section as desired and click **OK**.

The Rubber Stamp tool was one of the features that set Photoshop apart from other imaging applications, almost from the very beginning. It is unique compared to any other option we will examine in this section in that it allows you to brush a previous image version onto your existing image. The difference is subtle but powerful. The Layers, Fill, Paste, and Undo commands all apply their corrections globally, to the entire image or into a selected area. It is true that you can Paste into a selection, cut a mask, or do other things to control the areas being modified, but the end result is a time-consuming nonintuitive action. (The obvious exception is when you want to modify a hard-edged area.)

Rubber stamping lets you feel that the image is right at the tip of your brush and that you can apply as much or as little as you need (Figure 1.16). As a tool, the Rubber Stamp is selected through the toolbox, and is configured in the Rubber Stamp Options palette. You can access the Snapshot, Pattern, and From Saved data through the Options pop-up menu. Once the tool is configured, you can paint the various versions back into your design.

With the Clone option selected, the Rubber Stamp tool is like a pixel transport device; it takes pixels from one area, and replicates them in another area. With the Rubber Stamp tool selected, pressing **Option** allows you to specify the input point for the cloning. Any painting done after that will use the input point as a source for the pixel data, picking up pixel information from the source point and dropping it where the brushstroke dictates.

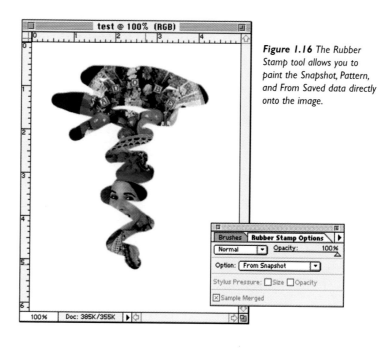

Figure 1.16 The Rubber Stamp tool allows you to paint the Snapshot, Pattern, and From Saved data directly onto the image.

The Rubber Stamp tool allows you to specify the input point to move with the cursor or to remain stationary. For example, when you select an input point and begin painting, Photoshop looks at the relationship between the source and the paint stroke. Let's say that the initial paint stroke began 2 inches diagonally from the input point. That grid relationship is remembered by Photoshop, and it can continually move the input to maintain that relationship between input point and paint stroke. Move the cursor up 4 inches, and the input point also moves up 4 inches, continuously reflecting the spatial relationship between input source point and paint stroke. This dynamic, movable input mode is referred to as the Rubber Stamp Align mode. Cloning and Pattern options both give the ability to specify Align or Non-aligned modes of painting in the image.

The Align mode maintains the proportional relationship between the cursor and input points, and the Non-align mode does the opposite. This translates into the input point automatically snapping back to the original point whenever the mouse button is released. This can be useful if you want to multiply the same object many times in an image, as the input point remains constant until a new one is set or until the tool is changed.

In the Clone modes, the Rubber Stamp looks only at the current image, and paints the data directly under the input point you specify. In the Snapshot, Pattern, or Saved modes, Photoshop paints the data currently housed in these areas at the corresponding input point.

In general, you can never have too many saved versions of your file, as long as you can get at them. The preceding examples of how to save multiple versions are a major component in building a safety net for an intuitive workflow.

Layers

Photoshop 3 introduced the use of layers as a means of isolating various image components, allowing full editing control at all times. Initially, saving a layer added a whopping 25% of the original file size to the image. At that rate, you would certainly think twice before adding very many layers because the system would slow to a crawl. Adobe has addressed this problem, and Photoshop layers are now much more frugal in how they add to the file size.

Photoshop now automatically creates a new layer each time you paste into an image. Saving versions or selections to a layer is a good thing to do, and it's never been easier. Selecting the entire image and choosing **Duplicate** from the Layers palette will create a new layer with a copy of your entire image. If you have a fast processor and a lot of RAM, this can be a good way to save and access various versions of your image.

Using Safety Nets

Please understand that saving to files, scratch disks, and layers are not isolated processes. They are interwoven, much like an actual net, and much like a net, they are stronger and more effective when they are combined. You can duplicate an image to a separate file, for example, and modify it with a filter effect. It can then be brought back into the original file as a separate layer, a copy of which is saved to the scratch disk. This allows the filtered layer to be modified, while the original layer can be brought back via a layer mask. The Rubber Stamp can also paint back the previous version of the filtered effect (Figures 1.17 A–D). The key is to know when it is most expedient to isolate an image or selection, either as a layer, or as a new file. Listed next are some typical scenarios for when to use which save area.

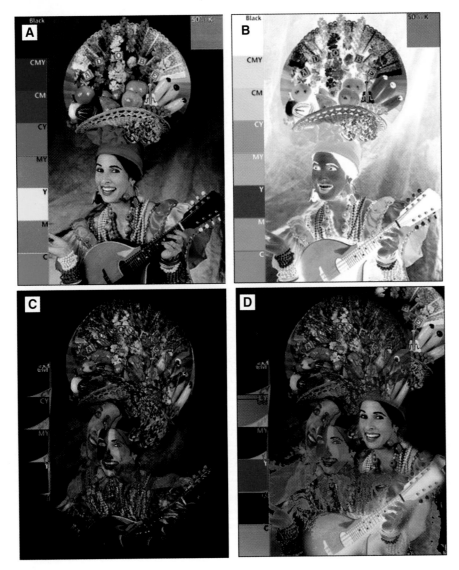

Figures 1.17 A–D
Combining data from multiple sources allows for the creation of a complex composite image. A-C are sources; D is the composite.

SAVING TO NEW FILES

Save to a new file when you need to modify an isolated area or selection. For example, a silhouetted product shot might be used in a number of different ways: as a pattern, as an abstraction, in a catalog, and in a montage. It would make sense to isolate it from the image into its own file, where it can be accessed for all its various duties.

It also makes sense to save when you want to make a local modification to one object or area. Rather than pay the penalty of long processing times for the entire image, save the area to be modified as a separate file, modify it to your liking, and bring it back in as a layer. This is especially effective for large files. You can take this logic a step further by reducing the separate file to 72 ppi and then making your changes. Also, 72 ppi matches the native resolution of most monitors, allowing you to see the image with good detail, while minimizing the file size. This will allow you to explore a number of various options or filter combinations quickly, just to get a sense of where you want to go with things. At that point you can create a separate file and apply the effect at full resolution.

SAVING

Remember that the Revert, Copy, Snapshot, Pattern, and Undo commands capture an entire image, which can be restored at a later time. Restoration is central to the process of intuitive workflow. Therefore, you should save multiple versions to these various areas at significant points in your design process. This determining factor could be that you really like the state of the image at that moment and want to be able to go back to if things get worse instead of better.

You might also want to save at a particular point because you are about to make radical changes to an image and you want to temper those changes with the current version. You can apply an effect full force and then soften it by bringing back some of the original image through the Snapshot or Revert commands. The significance of this point is underscored by the way many artists work. Consider how most people take a shower. When we get in the shower, we don't turn the temperature to one setting and just jump in. We tend to turn it on too hot, then temper it down a bit, and then add a bit more warm until it's just right. As designers, we do the same thing: we apply an extreme effect and then vary the opacity or intensity a bit until it's perfect.

Photoshop also offers a more linear way of softening an effect through the **Fade** command (Figure 1.18). Located under the Filter

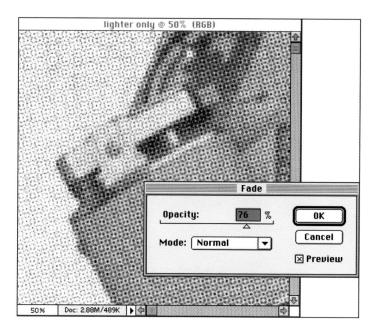

Figure 1.18 *The Fade slider allows you to soften the effects of the previous filter or color modification.*

menu, the Fade command lets you tone down the last applied effect by using a slider dialog box. Once an effect such as a filter or curve is applied, select Fade from the Filter menu and adjust the slider. Be sure that the Preview box is checked so that you can see the changes in real time. This lets you combine the effect with the original version in a very straightforward way. It does not preclude the use of the Snapshot or Revert commands, however, because these options allow you to bring back image information from other files or from long-forgotten steps.

LAYERS

Layers are like chocolate. If it didn't have calories, we just might eat a steady diet of nothing else. Unfortunately, after too much indulgence, we start to notice a bit more of us in the mirror than we want. Just as chocolate adds calories that make our bodies fat, layers add pixels that make our files fat. And fat files are slow and unresponsive when we ask them to do things. The trick, then, is to use layers until performance is not impacted beyond what you can bear. On a Power Mac 9500/120, that's about 90 MB total. At that point, things slow down,

and duplicating layers to separate files, merging them, or flattening the entire image becomes necessary (all of these functions can be accessed in the Layers pop-up menu).

If it weren't for the file-size issue, layers could probably solve all the problems in working with bitmap files. As mentioned before, you can save multiple file versions to different layers or isolate image components that can be moved about at will. You can also create patterns, control opacity between layers, and experiment with different effects without jeopardizing the entire composition.

Photoshop 4 has an Adjustment Layer feature that allows you to correct color and tone in all the layers below the adjustment layer without actually changing them. It acts like an overlay that the image, or even a single layer, can be seen through.

Layers are pretty easy to align with each other. This allows you to make multiple layers of the same image, modify the color in each, and combine them to get some great effects. Layers can also be used as reference materials. If you save image versions to the clipboard, as a pattern, as a snapshot, and in other areas, it can be hard to keep track of what's where. Save a version to a layer when you save to the scratch disk area. You can keep the layer turned off as you work and activate it as a reminder if you need to. While you can't change the resolution of a single layer, you can make the reference layers really small, so that they function as thumbnails.

These and other ideas are detailed in Chapter 4. Just remember that the layer is one type of safety net that you can construct to help you work more efficiently and intuitively.

Conclusion

If one is to work intuitively with Photoshop, then an optimized system is definitely a must. It will accelerate the pace and allow you to see various design decisions in closer context with each other. Following close behind an optimized system is the adoption of an intuitive strategy. It really can be similar to pixel juggling, as you keep a number of image versions active and "up in the air," through use of layers, other file sources, and the various storage areas. Understanding how each of these options facilitates a flexible and intuitive process will allow you to squeeze more out of the individual methods and steps in the chapters that follow.

RECIPE: — USING MULTIPLE APPLY MODES AND SOURCES

This exercise shows how a single image can be dramatically altered using no other source image than itself. Specifically, the approach will be to apply multiple treatments to the image, saving them to various areas within Photoshop. They will ultimately be recombined with the Rubber Stamp tool to compose the final image.

The examples here are chosen randomly, based on the image. You can substitute any kind of filter or image treatment in their place. The key thing to learn is the process of storing and recombining image data.

1. If you have not done so already, save the image. (Figure 1.19 shows my original.) This may sound obvious, but it is important because we will be relying on a revert from the last saved version. If your image is a new scan or has not been saved in its current state, you need to do that now.

2. Select **Image: Adjust: Invert** to invert the image.

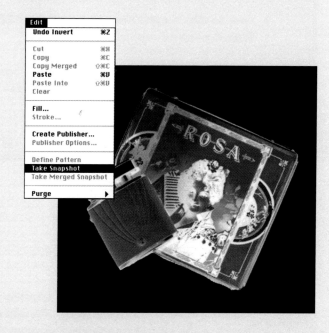

Figure 1.20
The inverted image saved to Snapshot.

Figure 1.19
The original image.

3. Once the effect is applied, select **Edit: Snapshot** to save the inverted image to the Snapshot area (Figure 1.20).

4. Select **Edit: Undo** Invert to go back to the original image. At this point you have the inverted image available in the Snapshot area and the original image available because it was saved.

5. Select **Image: Adjust: Hue/Saturation**. Click on the **Colorize** and **Preview** check boxes. Move the Hue slider to -110, the Saturation to 70, and the Lightness to -5. Click **OK** (Figure 1.21).

Figure 1.21 *Colorize the image.*

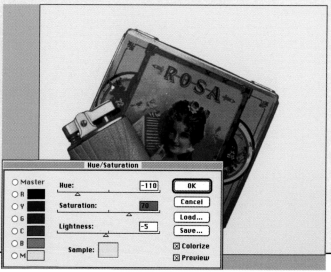

6. Once the effect is applied, choose **Select:All**. Select **Edit: Define Pattern** to save the entire image as a pattern.

7. Select **Edit: Fill**. Select **Saved** in the Contents Use pop-up menu, and **100%** and **Normal** in the Blending section (Figure 1.22). Click **OK** to fill with the original image.

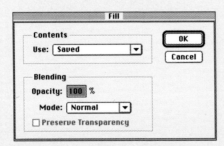

Figure 1.22
The Fill dialog box.

8. For one last effect, select **Filter:Texture:Texturizer**. Set the texture pop-up menu to Sandstone, scaling to 138%, relief at 14%, and Light Dir. to Top. Click **OK** to apply the texture effect (Figure 1.23). At this point you can paint the original image from the Revert command, the inverted image from the Snapshot command, the colorized image from the Pattern command. We will combine these versions with the existing texturized image to create a final composite.

Figure 1.23
Applying a texture to the image.

9. Select the Rosa case only (not the lighter), and choose **Fill** from the Edit menu. Select **Snapshot** from the Contents menu, leaving 100% and Normal selected in the Blending section. Click **OK** to fill the case with the inverted image, leaving the texture in the background and the lighter (Figure 1.24).

Figure 1.24 Fill the cigarette case with the inverted image.

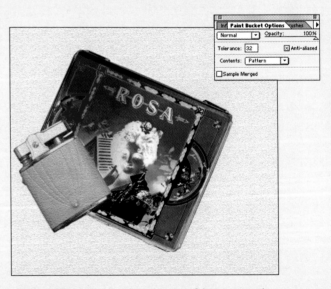

Figure 1.25 Painting the colorized version of the image into the borders of the case.

Figure 1.26 Painting from saved, using the Difference mode.

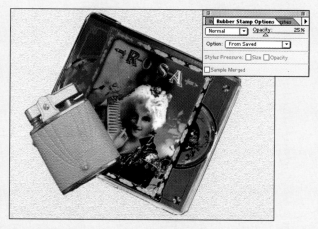

Figure 1.27 Restate the darks in the face, painting from saved using the Normal mode.

10. Double-click the Paint Bucket tool to activate the Options palette. Select **Pattern** from the Contents pop-up menu, leaving the other controls in their default state. Click in the border areas of the case to fill them with the purple colorized version of the image (Figure 1.25).

11. Double-click the Rubber Stamp tool and choose **From Saved** in the options menu and Difference as an apply mode. This will paint back a saturated version of the original image, as seen in the left of the figure. Paint the image as desired, reducing the Opacity slider to transition the effect (Figure 1.26).

12. Finish the image by choosing Normal as an apply mode and lightly painting the face back in (Figure 1.27). Vary the opacity here as well to feather the effect and intensify the contrast as needed (Figure 1.28).

Figure 1.28
The final image.

Chapter 2

INTUITIVE SELECTION SKILLS

When you look at an image, you do not see a grid of pixels with various colors and shapes, you see depth, space, and objects. You see tall mountains in the distance, a vase on a table, or maybe a tear in someone's eye. We impose our knowledge of the world on an image, and relate to digital images as though they were real. Our natural impulse when editing a digital image, is to reach in and grab that vase in order to change it. Because we can't really grab it, we at least want to isolate it to make changes.

Although these objects may seem real to us, they are very different to the computer's processor. To the computer, these objects are just pixels with various numeric values and positions. They are an arrangement of data and nothing more. A key component of becoming an advanced Photoshop user is being able to use its digital tools, which were designed for the lifeless pixel grid, to select areas in an image that mean something to us.

It is in our ability to isolate the old man's white hair, the texture on the back wall, or perhaps the green blanket in the corner that allow us to enhance the meaning of various images. For instance, we choose to emphasize one area or diminish another. In selecting and changing an image, we gain control over the composition and open up a world of possibilities.

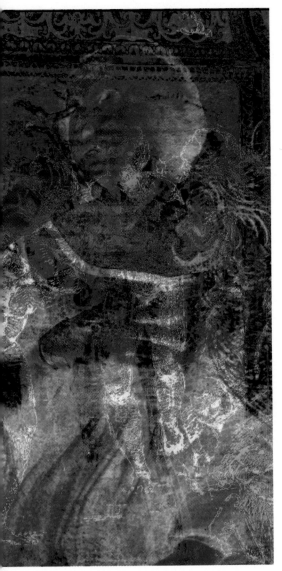

We impose our knowledge of the world on an image, and relate to digital images as though they were real.

Figures 2.1 A–D *Solid selection skills give tremendous control over the various image effects. A shows the original image; B contains added background effects; C exhibits collage effects, and D filter effects.*

Compositional Advantages

Good selection skills allow you to create compositions that have greater impact, focusing on the message you want to convey. With solid selection skills, you can seamlessly integrate an image into a background, explore object-based collage, or selectively enhance a poorly shot image.

You can also abstract a conventional image or graphic by adding filters or textures to certain areas. Good selection skills allow you to abstract certain areas of an image without losing the representational quality of the image (Figures 2.1 A–D).

Selection Types

What makes a good selection? At the risk of stating the obvious, a good selection is one that activates the pixels you want and ignores the ones you don't. Beyond this, the criteria will vary from image to image, depending on your intentions. In a naturalistic photograph, a good selection will have edges that smoothly transition into the non-selected areas. Hard-edged selections will not include any discolored edges that can halo the object against the background (Figure 2.2). If you are going for a collage look, edges will be clean and precise, even if they do succeed in giving a cut-out appearance.

Geometric Area Selections

Geometric selections usually have a hard-edged, linear shape. The most basic geometric selections are rectangles or squares. More com-

plex selections tend to be made up of line segments, and the most complex geometric selections have straight lines and curves. Generally speaking, any shape that can be created in a vector-based application, such as Adobe Illustrator, is a geometric selection.

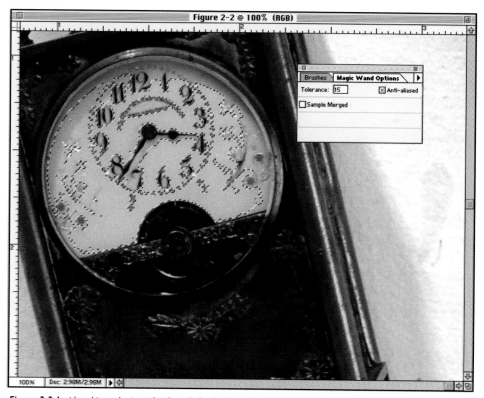

Figure 2.2 *Avoid making selections that have haloed edges or pixel artifacts. Take the time to clean things up.*

THE MARQUEE TOOL

The more basic geometric selections are created with the Marquee and Path tools. In addition, some geometric selections can be made with the Polygon Lasso tool. Selections made with these tools have very hard edges and don't deliver much control over details. They are perfectly suited for large geometric areas or graphic shapes.

The Marquee tools allow you to create rectangular or oval selections. When the **Shift** key is held down, the shape of the selection is constrained to a square or circle. You can also designate the proportions of the area to be selected by typing in a width-to-height ratio or by typing in specific pixel dimensions. As a handy tool for Web designers, Adobe even allows you to select an entire row or column of pixels.

The Marquee tool also allows you to crop an image as you drag a marquee. This has nothing to do with the selection options we've been discussing, but you will see that option listed as well.

All of these options can be selected from the Marquee Options palette, which can be chosen by double-clicking the tool or by selecting the tool if the Options palette is already active (Figure 2.3). You can also access the square, circle, and pixel row or column options by clicking and holding the triangle in the lower-right corner of the Marquee tool icon in the toolbox. The **M** key selects the square and circle marquee only. A pop-up menu provides access to these elements. One final selection option is to **Option**-click the Marquee tool, which cycles through the Oval, Rectangle, and Cropping tools.

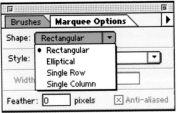

Figure 2.3 The Marquee tool offers a wide range of selection options.

Selections using the Marquee tools are usually not defined by the edges of an object, as a silhouette would be. Rather than following the contours of an object, these tools are used to isolate an area. Once selected, that area can be cropped or pasted into another image or file. These tools are also useful for creating vignetted borders or for creat-

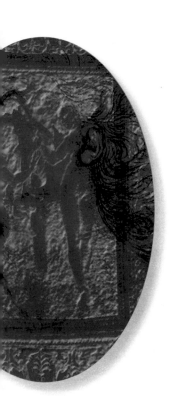

Figure 2.4 Marquee selection tools are perfect for selecting and softening blocks of an image to make text more readable.

ing buttons or borders for Web pages. For example, you might want to tone down a geometric area in an image to run text over it. These tools are perfect for such an application (Figure 2.4).

THE POLYGON LASSO TOOL

Selections using angled line segments can be created using the Polygon Lasso tool. This tool is available by **Option**-clicking the Lasso tool, through the pop-up menu in the Lasso Options palette or through the tool's pop-up menu via the triangle in the lower right corner of the Lasso tool icon. As an alternative, pressing L cycles

Figure 2.5 *The Polygon Lasso tool creates angular selections using straight line segments.*

Unless the selection is a quick and basic shape, you're probably better off creating paths and converting them to selections when you need them. As the next section shows, the Path tool is much more effective for any selection that the Polygon Lasso.

THE PATH TOOL

The Path tool is the most powerful and flexible of the geometric selection options. It can select almost any object with straight lines and curves, and the paths that result can be saved without adding much to the overall file size. Saving an actual selection through the Channels palette adds quite a bit to the file size, much as layers do.

Many experienced Photoshop users still seem to avoid the Path tool, which is why it will be discussed in some detail. Paths will keep your files small, give you the ability to create clipping paths, and share the exact same selection between different files. If you don't use Paths much, please take the time to familiarize yourself with what they can do.

through the Lasso options. This tool draws straight line segments that can be anchored by clicking at the desired spot in the image (Figure 2.5). You draw your segments and close the loop by joining the beginning and ending points. This tool does not allow you to draw Bezier curves like the Pen tool and is generally lacking in the control it offers the user. **Option**-clicking does change the tool to a freehand drawing mode, but that still does not add much precision to the selection process.

The Polygon Lasso tool is buried in Photoshop's tool set and is somewhat limited in its capabilities. Clicking the Polygon Lasso tool allows you to create points joined by line segments. The Polygon selection is ultimately closed at the point where it started, and the selection process in complete. Like the Polygon box tool in QuarkXPress, it is good for creating basic angular polygons, but you should think twice before trying to construct a detailed area with it.

Paths consist of points connected by linear segments. The Path tool does not actually make a selection as it is used. It creates a path, which is a linear description of an area within your image. Paths are not assigned to a specific layer, and they do not activate any pixels (like selections do), until you convert them to selections. Like the Pen tool in any draw program, you can create curves by clicking and dragging as you put points down on a path. These are related tools that add and subtract points from a path, convert corner points to curved ones, and move the finished path around the image. A path remains fluid and modifiable at all times.

The Path tools are located in the toolbox. The Pen tool is usually visible, but you can access the Selection tool, the Add and Subtract Points tool, and the Corner tool by clicking on the pop-up menu through the triangle at the lower right of the Pen tool icon (Figure 2.6). Option-clicking the icon also alternates through the tool list and P selects and cycles through tools.

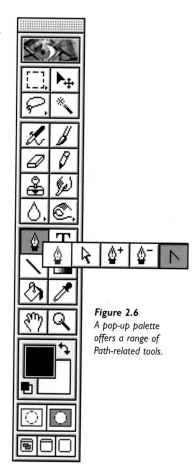

Figure 2.6
A pop-up palette offers a range of Path-related tools.

RECIPE: — CREATING DESIGNER BORDERS

Designer borders on images are all the rage these days. Stock photo catalogs abound with CDs full of image border patterns, emulating cut sheet film, roughened edges, and other textural or contextual designs. Designer borders are not hard to do. Once you understand the basic methodology there's no limit to the variations you can come up with.

The example that follows uses Photoshop's Spatter filter, but there are countless others. Experiment for yourself and get a sense of what works best for your style.

1. Open any image, select white as the background, and select **Canvas Size** from the Image menu. Increase the image height and width measurements to add a border around the image. For this 3-inch image, I added about 1/2 inch to each side. Be sure that the center square in the Anchor grid is selected, so that Photoshop adds the extra canvas evenly to all sides (Figure 2.7).

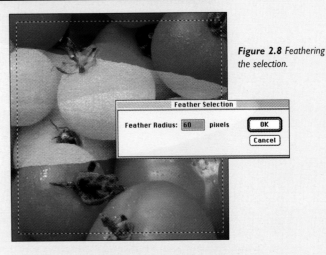

Figure 2.8 *Feathering the selection.*

3. Choose **Invert** from the Select menu, activating all of the pixels in the white border, fading slightly into the image. Select **Command/Control-H** to hide the edges of the selection.

4. Choose a filter that will apply a distinctive texture or surface variation. Remember to click on the minus symbol in the preview or to drag so you can see the image edge, in order to see the effect before it is applied. In this case, **Filter: Brush Strokes: Spatter** was selected. Set the Spray Radius to 25 and the Smoothness to 3 (Figure 2.9). Click **OK** to apply the effect to the image (Figure 2.10).

Figure 2.7 The Canvas Size dialog box,

2. Draw a marquee just inside the edge of the original image area and select **Feather** from the Select menu. The amount of feather you add will vary depending on the resolution of the image. In this case, 60 pixels were added, although the goal is to fade the selection in from the sides approximately 15% (Figure 2.8).

Figure 2.9 Invert the feathered selection and apply a filter.

Figure 2.10 *The final border effect.*

Figures 2.11–2.14
By varying the filters used, the border options are endless.

A few other examples are listed next to show more possibilities for this approach, all of which feature native Photoshop filters (Figures 2.11–2.14).

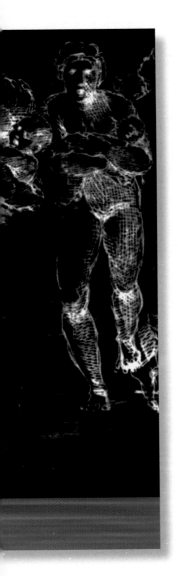

Once a path is created and saved, you can convert it to a selection with the Make Selection command in the Paths Options palette submenu. This is a great alternative to saving selections, which take up vast file real estate. An addition to converting paths to selections, the Paths palette submenu lets you name paths, activate and deactivate them, and copy and delete them. You can also convert a selection into a path by clicking on the Make Path button in the Paths palette.

In addition, you can stroke a path in the same way you stroke a selection and you can fill it with a color or pattern. The Paths options palette submenu is accessed through the small triangle in the upper-left corner of the palette (Figure 2.15).

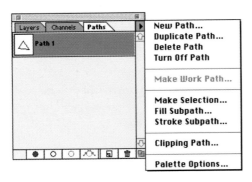

Figure 2.15 *The Paths palette submenu.*

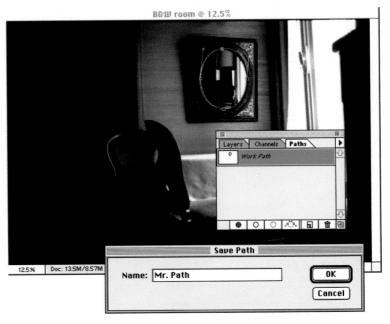

Figure 2.16 *Saving a path.*

The Paths palette represents each path as a bar running across the palette. From the time you click the first point to the time it is saved, it is called a Work Path. To save a Work Path, double-click the bar, name the path in the box that appears, and click **OK** (Figure 2.16). One other option that is not very well documented is the ability to copy paths from one file to another. To do this, simply open the source and destination files and drag the path bar from the paths palette onto the open window of the destination file. It is automatically copied over.

Clipping paths are paths that stay with the file as it is placed in illustration or layout programs. A clipping path will mask everything outside of the path, allowing only the inside area of the path to be seen. This is a godsend for those wishing to silhouette an object on a page or illustration.

To create a clipping path, first create the desired path and save it. Select **Clipping Paths** from the Paths palette pop-up menu. In the

dialog box that follows, select the desired path from the Paths pop-up menu. Specify the flatness of the path, which determines how closely the clipping path adheres to the complexity of the original path, and click **OK**. Clipping paths can only be saved with EPS files, so be sure to check the file type if a clipping path doesn't appear to be working as expected.

The Paths tools are perfect for selecting an object that is non-organic, yet somewhat complex. For example, a toaster or automobile would be perfect objects to select with the Paths tool. They are complex, yet they possess a certain symmetry. The collection of angles and balance are consistent enough to be handled with these tools. In contrast, you would never attempt to select a tree or a rushing river with the Path tool.

Organic Area Selections

Organic shapes, like the trees and rivers mentioned in the last paragraph, are natural objects that usually lack a symmetry or mathematical logic. Although chaos theorists and fractal mathematicians may disagree with that last statement, for the sake of this discussion an organic shape is one that is complex and somewhat unpredictable. Generally, if you're presented with the task of selecting an area and your first reaction is "How the heck am I going to select this?", you are probably looking at an organic shape.

If an object is difficult to select by its edge, it can usually be selected by its color or value. The tree mentioned earlier probably has green leaves, or the stream may have a blue hue to the water. Much of your success in selecting organic objects will be in your ability to isolate colors or hues from the surrounding objects in the image and select them as you need to.

THE MAGIC WAND

The Magic Wand is the most useful tool for selecting colors or values in an image. When clicked on an image, it selects all of the adjoining pixels based on the value of the original pixel. Click on a green pixel,

and you select all of the adjoining green pixels, regardless of how irregular the green shape may be (Figure 2.17).

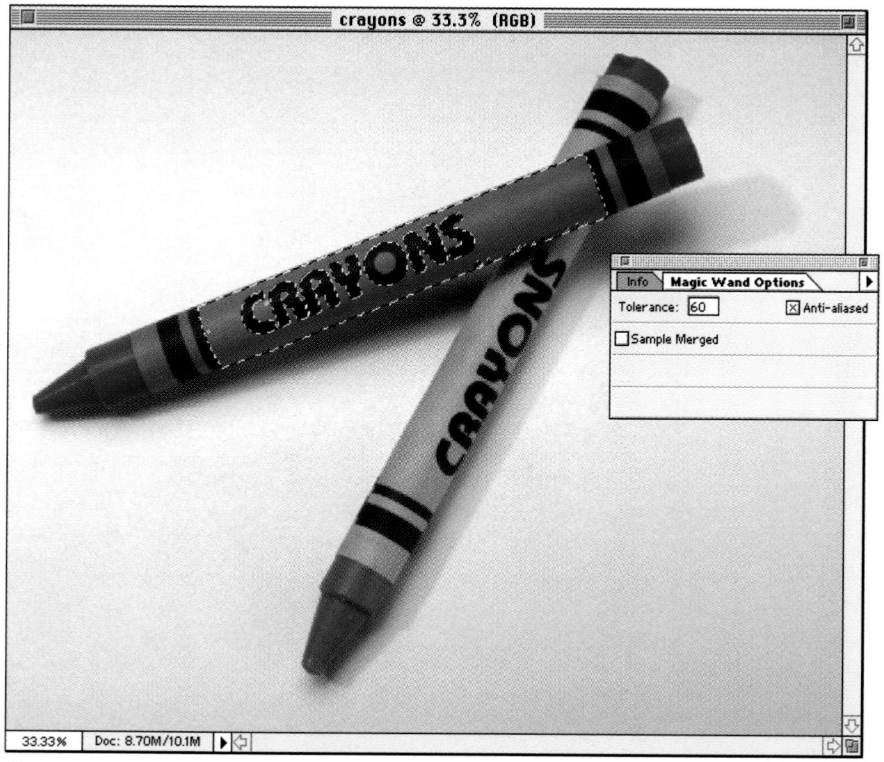

The Magic Wand also has a tolerance feature that discerns exactly how much it should deviate from the original pixel value selected. You can set the values to just one or two, which would select only the exact green pixel value selected, or you can move the tolerance as high as 255, which would select all of the adjoining pixels that even remotely resemble a green value. Since pixels values only go as high as 255, it is impossible for the tolerance setting to go beyond this point.

To change the Magic Wand's tolerance setting, double-click on the Magic Wand tool so that the Options palette appears (Figure 2.18). At that point, you can type in the tolerance value you need for the task at hand. By manipulating the tolerance, you can select an amazing range of objects that would be very difficult to select otherwise. An object that has been anti-aliased, for example, would be very tough to select with the other tools. The way the edges feather off into the background can be captured if you experiment with the right tolerance setting. If fact, any area of graduated tone can be selected with the Magic Wand tool when set at the right tolerance.

Graduated tones and feathered areas aren't the only areas for the Magic Wand. If you have a large area of solid color, like an object against a white background, it's a simple matter to use the Magic Wand with a tolerance of five or less. With one click on the background, you can select the entire area.

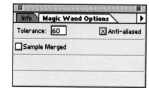

Figure 2.18 The Magic Wand Options palette.

THE LASSO TOOL

The Lasso tool is something of a hybrid tool, allowing more of an organic feel than the Paths or Marquee tools, yet acting more rigid than the Magic Wand. With the Lasso tool, you click and drag to draw the area you want to select, closing the loop between the starting and end points of your selection. If you release the mouse before you join the beginning and end points, Photoshop draws a straight line between them.

Because it relies almost entirely on the human hand and eye to make its selection, the Lasso tool is less effective in precision selections. It can be useful in start-

Figure 2.17 With the proper tolerance setting, the Magic Wand can select almost any color-based area.

32

ing a selection that will be manipulated in some other way (see "Fine Tuning Selections"), or in making a more expressionistic or gestural selection.

Color-Based Selections

This chapter began by stating that a good selection is one that activates the pixels you want while ignoring the rest. Having looked at the edges and areas of an image, about the only thing left to explore is the color. Photoshop makes it very simple to modify the color of an image, selectively within an object or globally across the entire screen.

With these controls, you can select a blue crayon out of a pile of other crayons and change it to a green one. The sky can become overcast and gray. The light can change from morning yellow to midday white. A tree can change from the green of June to the rust colors of September (Figures 2.19 A, B). There are more utilitarian uses as well. For example, all of the out-of-gamut colors in your image can come back into gamut without disrupting any other color relationships.

Photoshop allows you to select all of the pixels in your image that have the same RGB or CMYK values. The Color Range command selects pixels of common value throughout the entire image. Let's say you are trying to select a red apple. Selecting the red pixels may delineate the apple, but you may be surprised to find that the shadows in the corner of your image also contain a lot of red that has also been selected. It is usually a simple matter of modifying your selection accordingly, excluding the

unwanted pixels from your selection (see "Modifying Your Selection").

USING COLOR RANGE

The Color Range command in the Select menu is the main area for making color-based selections and modifications. You can select by colors or tones, or just use this command to get a good look at the color distribution in your image (Figure 2.20). Because colors can hide where you least expect them, you should take a minute to look at an image and understand exactly where the color information is. With a clear picture of how the color is distributed, you will have a better idea of how to modify your image.

When you open the Color Range dialog box, you are presented with a preview window, a Select pop-up menu, and a Selection Preview option. If Sampled Colors is active in the Select menu, then the Fuzziness slider also activates, which acts like a tolerance setting for the colors sampled in the image. To look at how color is distributed in the image, set the Selection Preview pop-up menu at the bottom of the dialog box to White Matte. This will make everything in the image (not the preview window) turn white, except for the color being evaluated. With White Matte selected, click and hold on the Select pop-up menu, and drag down to Reds. This will show you all of the reds in your image. You can go down the line, looking at red, green, blue, as well as cyan, magenta, and yellow. This is effective in that you can see how color is distributed regardless of what color model you're in. In addition, it shows the results as the color or value being evaluated, rather than the grayscale image you see when you evaluate channels information.

Figure 2.19 A and B Color-based selections allow you to dramatically alter an image. A shows the selection before color alterations were made. B shows the resulting image.

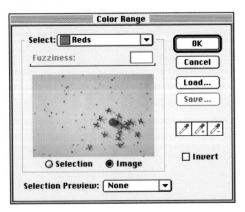

Figure 2.20 The Color Range dialog box.

In examining the highlights, midtones, and shadows in an image, the areas selected show up in their respective colors. This is the fastest and easiest way to get a sense of where the color is in your image, which is the first step in knowing how to make a color-based selection (Figures 2.21 A–D).

Hopefully, one of the colors or tones in the Select pop-up menu reflects the color range you want to select. If not, you can use the following steps to fine-tune your color selection (Figure 2.22):

1. Choose the Sampled Colors setting in the Select pop-up menu.
2. Click on the eyedropper icon beneath the Save button.
3. Click on the color in your image you wish to select.
4. Adjust the Fuzziness slider to isolate the exact range of color desired.
5. Use the eyedropper to add or subtract colors to the selected range.

The Sampled Colors approach works much like the Magic Wand selection option, in that an area is defined with a click, depending on its tolerance. One difference between the Magic Wand and the Color Range function is that Color Range selects all of the pixels of a certain value, rather than just the contiguous ones. The Color Range approach is much more intuitive and can be very useful when extra precision is required.

Figures 2.21 A–D
Color Range allows you to make image selections based on the highlight, midtone, and shadow areas in an image. A shows the original image; the highlights, midtones, and shadows are examined in B, C, and D.

Figure 2.22 *Fine-tuning the color selection.*

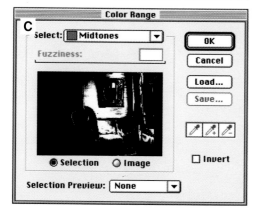

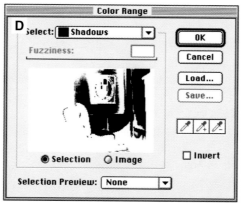

RECIPE: — THREE SELECTION STRATEGIES

Master Selection Techniques

Although it doesn't deliver a finished product, this recipe can empower you. The fact that Photoshop provides so many ways of selecting an object underscores the importance of selections in the Photoshop creative process. It all starts with selections, and if those skills are lacking, then everything else suffers.

This recipe will explain how to select an object through LAB channels, through threshold commands, and through the oversaturation of specific colors or layers.

Threshold

The image of rippling water presents a real challenge with so much subtle variation of tone that it is hard to decide where or what to select

(Figure 2.23). The Threshold command makes this selection issue much easier.

1. Duplicate the entire image to a separate layer by selecting **Duplicate Layer** from the Layers Palette Options menu.
2. Activate the copied layer and select **Image: Adjust: Threshold**. With the Preview box checked, Threshold converts the entire image to either black or white pixels. The Threshold level determines which pixels turn black and which ones turn white, and is controlled by moving the white slider beneath the histogram. Adjust the slider until you see a desirable selection area, and click **OK** (Figure 2.24).
3. Select the Magic Wand tool and click in the white or black area to define a selection. If you want all of the white areas in the image,

Figure 2.23 The original image.

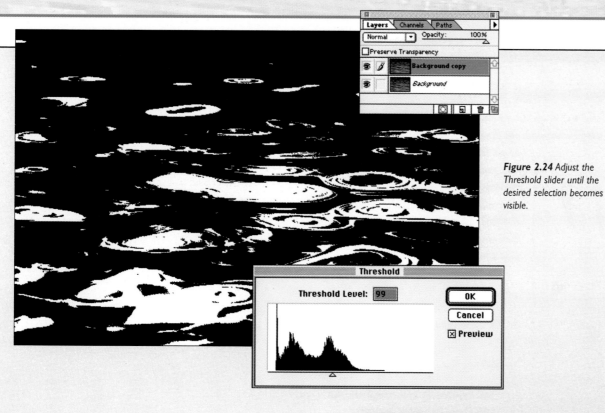

Figure 2.24 *Adjust the Threshold slider until the desired selection becomes visible.*

Figure 2.25 *Adjust curves to achieve the final effect.*

select the **Similar** command from the Select menu. In this example, all of the white pixels in the image were used as a selection.

4. Delete the copied layer, and the selection will remain active over the original image, ready to be modified. Because the Threshold slider applies some hard edges, you may want to soften the selection by applying the **Feather** command from the Select menu. In this example, an 8-pixel feather was applied to the image.

5. The yellow/green glowing effect was achieved by raising the RGB curve in the light gray 1/4 tones from 197 to 222, lowering the Blue curve from 190 to 112, and raising the Green channel from 164 to 222 Figure 2.25 shows the final image.

RECIPE: — CONTINUED

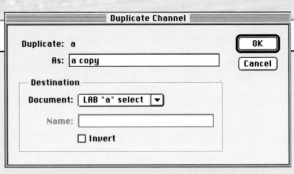

Duplicate Channel

Duplicate: a

As: a copy

Destination

Document: LAB "a" select ▼

Name:

☐ Invert

OK

Cancel

Figure 2.28 *Duplicate the "a" channel to a new channel.*

Selections through Channels

With all of the red and magenta speckled through this flower image, selecting the entire flower with the Magic Wand or Path tool could be tough (Figure 2.26). You could paint it via Quick Mask or use the Lasso, but nothing really seems to be a clear approach. At times like this, remember to check out individual channels to see if there is any tonal separation that you can take advantage of.

Figure 2.26 *The original image.*

1. Although the RGB channels show little promise, the LAB colorspace presents an opportunity (Figure 2.27). Once an image is converted to LAB, (**Image: Mode: LAB Color**), the "a" channel, which represents the relationship between green and red, shows the entire area of the flower as a light gray.

2. Select the **"a" channel** from the Channels palette, and **Duplicate Channel** from the Options menu. Name the new channel and click **OK**. This creates a separate channel with the grayscale values contained in the "a" channel (Figure 2.28).

3. With only the "a" channel selected, select **Image: Adjust: Curves**. Lower all of the mids and shadows from 0 to 88 to flat black. Conversely, raise all of the lighter tones from 154 to 255 to flat white. The result is a perfect white shape representing the flower (Figure 2.29).

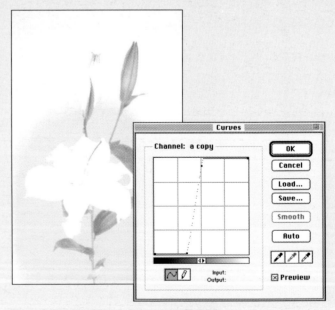

"a" Channel   "b" Channel   Lightness Channel

Figure 2.27 *The three LAB channels are Lightness, "a," and "b."*

Figure 2.29 *Adjust Curves to bring out the flower shape.*

4. While still in the "a" channel, set the Magic Wand to a tolerance of 5 and select the flower.

5. Reselect the composite channel, and change the color in the flower by selecting **Image: Adjust: Hue/Saturation** and modifying the color as desired (Figure 2.30). The settings used in the example were Hue 67, Saturation +17, and Lightness -6.

Figure 2.31 *The original image.*

Figure 2.30 *Changing the color of the flower.*

2. Click on the red of the watermelon to select that color. Adjust the range of selection with the Fuzziness slider. You will see that the image itself reflects the selection, thanks to the White Matte option. Click **OK** to accept the selection.

3. Select the **Hue/Saturation** command and click the **Colorize** button to shift the color in the selected area. The settings shown here are Hue 90, Saturation 100, and Lightness +19 (Figure 2.33).

Figure 2.32 *Use Color Range to sample a color-based area.*

Figure 2.33 *The final image.*

Color Range

With bright colors, as in this pile of fruit (Figure 2.31), remember to try to select by color via the Color Range. These distinct colors are easily selected with this command.

1. Choose **Color Range** from the Select menu. Select **Sampled Colors** from the Select menu, **White Matte** as a Selection Preview, and click on the **Image** radio button. (Figure 2.32).

A

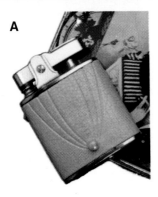

B

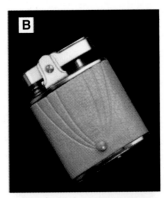

C

Fine-Tuning Selections Like a Pro

One of the requisites for making selections like a pro is patience. You need to approach certain selections with the mind-set that the selection might just take a while. Although patience is key, it is also important to understand how to combine the various selection tools, which can save time and to make things easier.

The basics for combining selections is knowing that you can hold down the **Shift** key to add to a selection, and that holding down the **Option** key subtracts from the selection. With that basic information, you are able to begin a selection with the Magic Wand to select a general area, then switch to the Lasso, holding down the **Shift** key as you drag around the smaller noise segments that were not selected by the wand. This cleans up the selection much faster than trying to click on each little noise segment with the wand. You could also select **None** (**Command-D**) and adjust the Magic Wand tolerance to select more of the area, depending on the image.

The important thing is to realize that each selection tool has its own strengths. By combining them you are able to select virtually any object or area. In addition to selection tools, Photoshop offers selection modifiers, which allow fine-tuning of an existing selection. Listed next are the selection modifiers with brief descriptions of how they operate.

Using the Feather Command

The Feather command softens the edges of the current selection, fading them into the unselected area. It allows you to anti-alias a selection by at least a pixel or two, hiding any mistakes that may have occurred in the selection process. You may even want to vignette a section such as a box or oval, creating a more dramatic fade-out of the selection (Figure 2.34 A–C).

Access the Feather dialog box by scrolling to the Feather command in the Selection menu. It will ask you to specify the amount of the feather in pixels. You should have some idea of the dimension of your image in pixels, allowing you to specify an accurate value. Type in the number and click **OK** to apply the feather. Don't be surprised if

Figure 2.34 *A The original image. The same selection, with B hard and C feathered edges.*

the flashing selection line shrinks more than you thought it would. The selection does extend beyond the dotted line on the screen, it just begins fading out at that point.

Using the Grow and Similar Commands

The Similar command from the Select menu activates all of the pixels with values similar to those currently selected. The amount selected with this command is dependent on the tolerance setting in the Magic Wand Options palette (Figure 2.35). Just like the Magic Wand, the higher the tolerance setting, the more pixels will be selected.

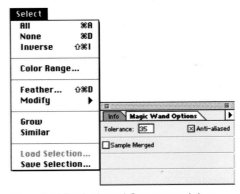

Figure 2.35 *The Similar and Grow commands base their selection range on the tolerance setting in the Magic Wand Options palette.*

This is a great way to select a specific color, either in an abstract pattern or an organic shape, and to select all of its occurrences in the image. Once selected, you can tweak the color or change it dramatically.

The Similar command is a cousin of the Grow command. Using the same tolerance settings as the Magic Wand, the Grow command expands the selected image based on the adjoining pixels. In other words, if the adjoining pixels to the selection would be included if a tolerance of 32 were selected, they are added to the selection. When the contrast between the original selection and the adjoining area becomes greater than the tolerance setting, the selection stops.

RECIPE: THE BLACK-AND-WHITE TV SCREEN

This effect emulates the look of an old black-and-white TV screen, and it can be used to create a graphic or documentary effect. Here's how to use it:

1. The first task is to create a line grid that will give the feel of a TV screen. Although you can import lines from a drawing program, it's not very difficult to add them through Photoshop. Begin by creating a new layer and turning off the main image so the blank layer with the checkerboard is all that is showing. You should also be in Full Screen Mode with Menu Bar, with Guides showing, and Snap to Guides active (remember that rulers must be showing to drag guides). Drag four guides around the edge of the image frame to help align the line grid as it is drawn (Figure 2.36).

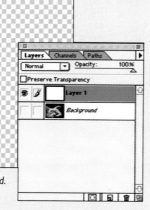

Figure 2.36 Begin on a blank layer to make the line grid.

2. Use the Path tool to draw one line horizontally across the top. Copy and paste the line repeatedly until five are equally spaced. Use the checkerboard grid to help with vertical spacing. Copy all five and paste them again, now stacking groups of five lines at a time. Repeat this process until the entire screen is full of horizontal path lines. Use the rulers to help you with spacing, and be sure to zoom in to 100% to ensure accuracy. The spacing used for this 4 X 7-inch 300 dpi image was 16 lines per inch.

3. Save the path, naming it **Grid** and click **OK**. Once the path is saved you may delete the new layer; it was only created to help in the creation of the grid.

4. Create a new channel and activate it, hiding the rest of the image.

5. With the new channel active, switch to the Paths palette and click on the **Grid** path in the Paths palette to activate it.

6. Double-click the Airbrush tool and select a 5 pixel soft brush with a pressure setting of 100%. Set the foreground color to white.

7. In the Paths palette, select **Stroke Path** from the Paths Palette Options menu (Figure 2.37). The dialog will reflect the last tool used, which should be the Airbrush settings you just specified. Click **OK** and Photoshop will stroke the path named Grid with the airbrush into the new channel.

Figure 2.37 With the path selected and a new channel active, select Stroke Path from the options menu.

8. Activate the main RGB channel and Select the entire image. Hold down the **Command-Option-Shift** keys and click on the grid channel to intersect the grid selection with the entire image. Set the background to white and delete the grid selection (Figure 2.38).

9. Choose **Select All** from the Select menu, and select **Filter: Blur: Gaussian Blur**. Set the Radius at 3.2 pixels, and click **OK** (Figure 2.39).

RECIPE: CONTINUED

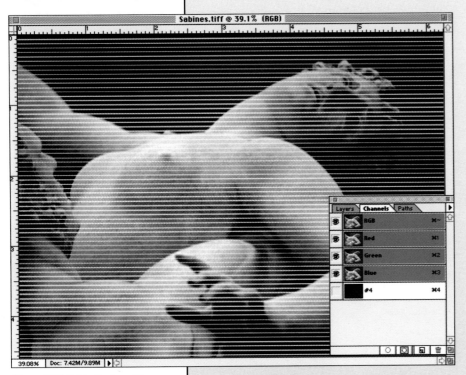

Figure 2.38 Delete the line grid selection from the main image.

8. Select **Image: Adjust: Hue/Saturation**. Click the **Colorize** checkbox, and set the Hue slider at -171, the Saturation at 77, and the Lightness at +10 (Figure 2.40).

9. Select **Filter: Noise: Add Noise**. Set the Amount slider to 50 and Uniform in the Distribution section. Click **OK** (Figure 2.41).

10. Select **Filter: Render: Lighting Effects**, Leave the light type on Spotlight, and adjust the intensity and focus to create a hot spot in the center of the image that darkens slightly at the corners. Keep the Properties sliders stationary. You can bump up the Exposure slider a

bit if the image calls for it (Figure 2.42). Click **OK** to apply the effect.

11. Set the background color to black and select **Canvas Size** from the Image menu. Enlarge the canvas dimensions to create a thin strip all around the image, making sure that the Anchor section remains in the center of the grid. Click **OK** to apply the border.

12. If handled with subtlety, a slight lens flare can be an excellent final touch. To apply it, select **Filter: Render: Lens Flare**. Set the Brightness slider to 46%, the Lens type at 105mm Prime, and move the Flare Center around the preview by dragging the + point (Figure 2.43). Once the effect is applied, consider toning it down with the Fade Command in the Filter menu. This can give just the right amount of control over the light intensity (Figure 2.44).

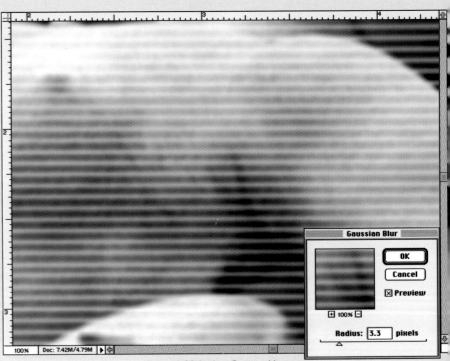

Figure 2.39 Apply a Gaussian blur.

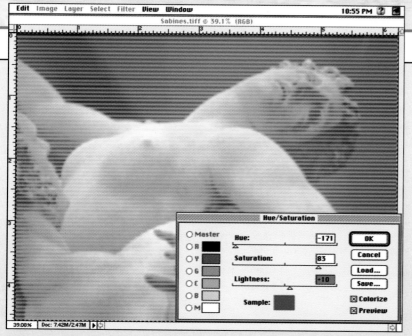

Edit Image Layer Select Filter View Window   10:55 PM

Figure 2.40 *Colorize the image.*

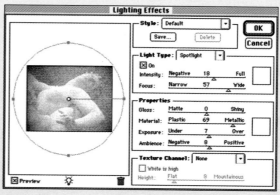

Figure 2.42
The lighting effects filter darkens the image at the corners.

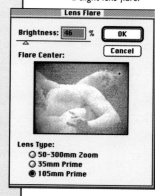

Figure 2.43 *Adding a slight lens flare.*

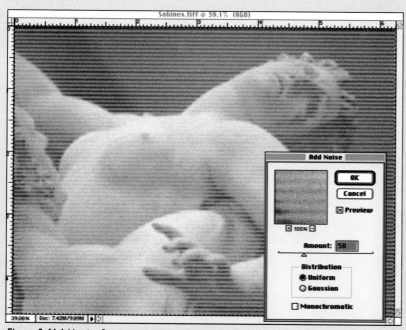

Figure 2.41 *Add noise for a snowy texture.*

Figure 2.44 *The final image.*

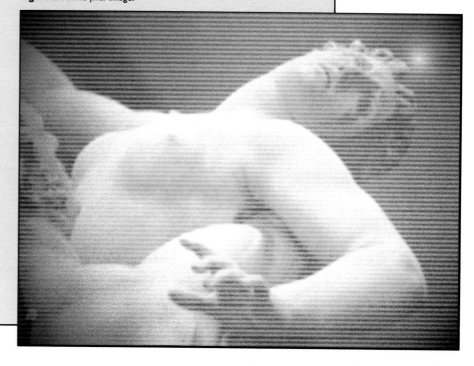

Using the Modify Options

Under the Select menu there is a group of selection modifiers under the Modify command. These commands are somewhat specialized, but you should know their purpose (Figure 2.45). The Border command allows you to transform an area selection into a border selection of a specified thickness. The Expand or Contract commands grow or shrink a selection by a specific number of pixels, while the Smooth command rounds the edges of a selection. All of these commands are limited to 16 pixels or less in value.

Using Quick Mask for Intuitive Selections

With a selection started, it can be very effective to employ Photoshop's Quick Mask feature. By clicking the Quick Mask icon

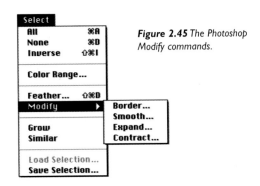

Figure 2.45 The Photoshop Modify commands.

below the color selection swatches, the currently selected area is represented by a colored mask. By double-clicking the Quick Mask icon, you can define the parameters of this feature, setting the mask color, its opacity, and whether the selected or unselected areas is covered by the mask (Figure 2.46).

Figure 2.46 The Quick Mask dialog box.

Advanced Quickmask Techniques

Most people use Quick Mask in a limited way, as they paint in a bit of edge here or erase a section there. Stop for a moment to experiment with all of the power that Quick Mask provides. Here are some of the effects you can explore:

- Use the Airbrush with various pressure settings to feather edges and add transparency or opacity to the selection. The mask will actually paint in lighter or darker to indicate an opaque selection or a transparent one. The result is a soft, feathered effect that can be created by hand.

- With the foreground and background colors set to black and white, use the Gradient tool to draw a gradient across the image. This results in a selection that fades out slowly. The gradient approach modifies the image more globally and is less specific to objects or image areas.

- Select the **Type** tool and click on the image to create a starting point for a text selection. When the Type dialog box appears, enter the words you want, select the font, size, and other details; click **OK**. The message you type appears as a part of the mask, and it is converted to a text-based selection when you exit the Quick Mask mode.

- Use the Sharpen and Blur tools to modify the edges of the Quick Mask. You can also use the Smudge tool to smear the Quick Mask and its associated selection.

- The Toning tool intensifies or minimizes the Quick Mask, depending on its settings. Experiment with the various controls in the Options palette to explore how they affect the mask.

In the Quick Mask mode, Photoshop's edit tools edit only the mask, not the actual pixels in the image. This means you can add to the mask with all of Photoshop's draw or paint tools or subtract from the mask with the erase tools. Once you have fine-tuned the mask, click out of the Quick Mask mode to convert the mask back to a selection. This is a terrific way to clean up edges in a selection, or to fill in the exact area needed. If you are more comfortable coloring something in and working with the paint tools, the Quick Mask feature will seem a lot more intuitive.

How to Save Selections

You've combined selection tools to select the perfect area. You've gone to Quick Mask to tweak the opacity, and the resulting selection gives you perfect control for the effect you're after. After all that work, how do you save the image so that you have it for the next time you need it? This is an important step in creating intuitive workflow, as you will frequently be going back and making further modifications as the piece develops.

There are many ways to save selections for future use. The appropriate method depends on how often you need access to the selection, your file size, and the type of selection.

When considering the selection type, you should evaluate whether it is essentially linear, tonal, or color-based. For example, a selection with well-defined edges would fall into the linear category, while an image of a misty field with soft, undefined edges would be essentially tonal. A color-based selection would follow the guidelines discussed previously.

Saving to Paths

If a selection is linear, it should be saved as a path whenever possible. It has already been mentioned that a path can be converted to a selection, but it is also possible to convert a selection to a path. The advantages to this are that a path adds very little to the overall file size, and can be easily stored and moved from file to file.

To save a selection as a path, go to the Paths palette submenu and select Make Work Path (Figures 2.47 A–C). The box that appears will ask you to define a tolerance, measured in pixels. The tolerance defines how closely the path will follow the selection. The default setting of 2 pixels is usually more than enough. Be careful not to convert a selection that is too detailed or too transparent, as the results can be less than acceptable. Once the path is created, it can be saved and stored, following the procedures outlined earlier.

Saving to Channels

Photoshop uses channels to separate and store color information in an image. In an RGB image, for example, all of the red information is in

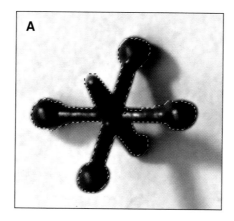
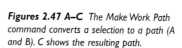
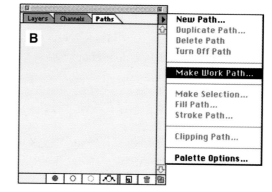

Figures 2.47 A–C *The Make Work Path command converts a selection to a path (A and B). C shows the resulting path.*

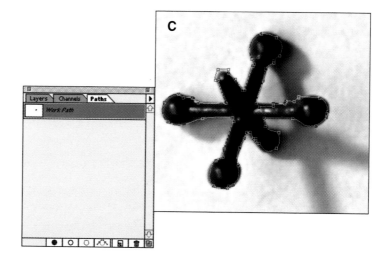

one channel, with the green and blue in their respective channels. Viewed separately, a color channel is represented as a grayscale image, with the highest concentration of color in the lightest or darkest areas (depending if the image is RGB or CMYK).

Whenever you employ the Save Selection command in the Select menu, the selection is saved as an additional channel (Figure 2.48). Channels are excellent places for selections that vary in opacity. If you have a gradient selection, one with a feathered edge or with varying opacity, saving to a channel will usually preserve most or all of the nuance in the selection.

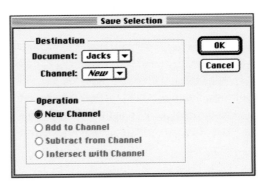

Figure 2.49 The Save Selection dialog box.

One advantage of the Save Selection command is that it gives you the option of saving the selection to another document. This command also gives the latitude of saving the selection as a new channel, or integrating it into an existing channel. This is done as an addition, subtraction, or intersection with the channel. To use the Save Selection command, select **Save Selection** from the Select menu, and designate the document you wish to save to in the Document pop-up menu in the Destination section. It will usually be the same one you're in at the time, but if another document is desired, be sure it is open for it to appear in the pop-up menu. If you are integrating the selection with an existing channel, you can designate the channel to be modified in the Channel pop-up menu in the same section (Figure 2.49).

Once a selection is saved as a channel, it can be reloaded through the Load Selection command in the Select menu. The Load Selection dialog box is virtually identical to the Save Selection dialog, with the additional feature that it allows you to invert the selection as it is activated. Other than that, the Destination and the Channel Interaction options look the same. In adding, subtracting, or intersecting a channel with a selection, the active selection at the time is modified by the channel information being loaded. This is the reverse of the process when saving a selection to a channel.

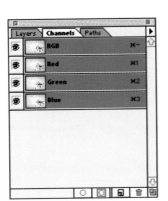

Figure 2.48 When a selection is saved, Photoshop creates a grayscale channel, visible through the Channels palette.

THE CHANNELS PALETTE

Photoshop delivers full control over channels through the Channels palette. The Channels palette submenu allows deleting, duplicating, and modification of the channels in a document. One interesting option is the Split Channels command, which separates the document into separate grayscale documents, one for each color and selection channel. This feature comes at the loss of your original color document, so make sure you're working from a copy before you select this option.

Conclusion

Knowing how to select an object convincingly is an integral component in creating intuitive workflow. If you have well-honed selection tools, you have the feeling that there's nothing you can't accomplish in Photoshop. On the other hand, poor selection skills will cause you to spend a lot of time figuring out work-around solutions for the effects you want to achieve. This is about as far removed from an intuitive workflow strategy as possible.

Selections should come quickly as you're working, and your ability to store and retrieve these selections will save you from reinventing the wheel. You should intuitively understand how to combine the various selection techniques in Photoshop, as most complex selections require a combination of moves before the final selection is realized.

Don't go any further until you're comfortable with the selection options outlined in this chapter. They aren't difficult once you understand them.

RECIPE: — DAY INTO NIGHT

In this recipe, the goal is to change the time of day in an image going from the light of midday to the shadows of evening. The challenges in doing this are the shifting color of light, the way reflections changes as intensity diminishes, and the way surfaces catch and resist light based on its direction and strength. The initial image is a midday Parisian street, with a strong architectural center that should cast some great shadows (Figure 2.50).

1. Begin by isolating the corner area that will go darkest as the scene shifts to night. Begin with a Marquee selection from the top down to the ground. Finish the selection by activating Quick Mask mode and airbrushing and feathering the selection into the lighter areas of the image. A 400 pixel brush did most of the work here, with varying pressure from 6% to 44% (Figure 2.51).

Figure 2.50 *The original image.*

Figure 2.51 *Airbrushing the final selection area in Quick Mask mode.*

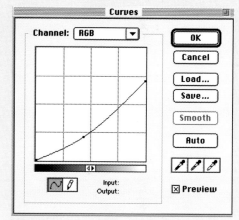

Figure 2.52
Adjust the curves to darken the right corner.

2. With the area selected, select **Image: Adjust: Curves** and lower the RGB composite making the input/output values read **255: 182**, and **111: 53** (Figure 2.52).

3. Double-click the Burn tool to activate its options palette. Vary the brush size and exposure to punch the darks at the top and in the corners (Figure 2.53).

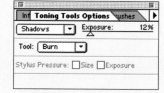

Figure 2.53 *Use the Burn tool to deepen the darkest areas.*

RECIPE: — **CONTINUED**

4. Colors often saturate as it gets dark. To emulate this effect, invert the selection by selecting **Invert** from the Select menu. Choose **Image: Adjust: Hue/Saturation,** and increase the Saturation to +34 and the Lightness to -31. (Figure 2.54).

5. To darken the upper left corner, save the current selection by selecting **Save Selection** from the Select menu. This saves the selection to a separate channel, automatically naming it #4. In the Channels palette activate the new channel and select white as the foreground color and black as the background color. Draw a gradient from the upper left corner down toward the center of the image (Figure 2.55).

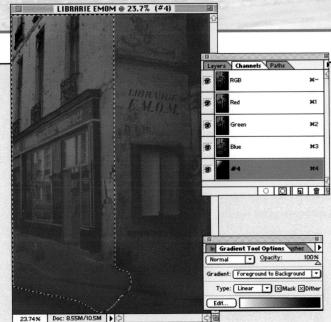

Figure 2.55 Drawing a selection gradient in a separate channel.

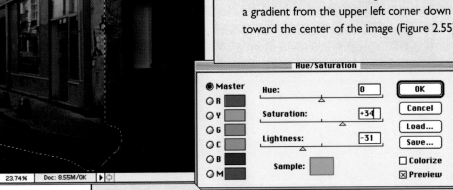

Figure 2.54
Saturate the colors in the storefronts.

Figure 2.56 Modify the Blue channel curve to add a glow to the storefront window.

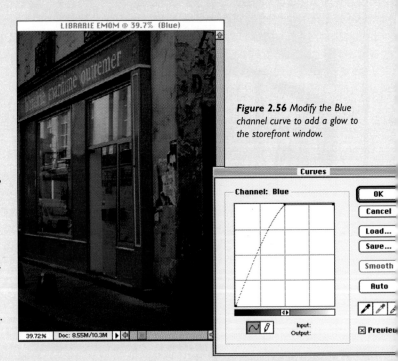

6. Activate the RGB composite channel again and select **Image: Adjust: Curves**. Modify the RGB composite curve with 2 points, making the input/output values read **255: 150, 126: 0**. This will darken the upper corner and give more of a feeling of nightfall.

7. Select the Polygon Lasso tool and draw around the square window frames to select them. Hold down the **Shift** key as you go from one window to the next, selecting all window areas at once.

8. Activate the Blue channel only, while keeping all channels visible. Select **Image: Adjust: Curves**. Modify the Blue curve with 1 point, making the input/output values read **128: 255** (Figure 2.56).

9. Select the Airbrush tool and change the apply mode to Multiply, with the pressure at 14%. Option click on the darkest areas of

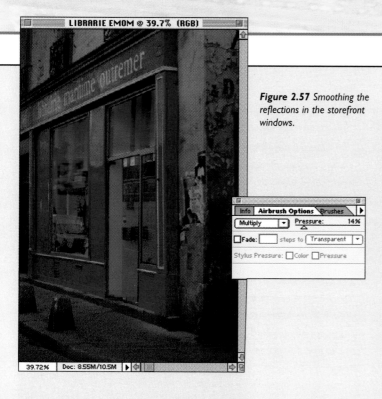

LIBRARIE EMOM @ 39.7% (RGB)

39.72% | Doc: 8.55M/10.5M

Figure 2.57 *Smoothing the reflections in the storefront windows.*

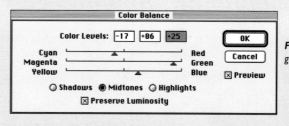

Color Balance

Color Levels: -17 +86 +25

Cyan ——————— Red
Magenta ——————— Green
Yellow ——————— Blue

○ Shadows ● Midtones ○ Highlights
☒ Preserve Luminosity

OK
Cancel
☒ Preview

Figure 2.59 *Adding a green fluorescent cast.*

Info | Airbrush Options | Brushes
Multiply ▾ Pressure: 14%
☐ Fade: ☐ steps to Transparent ▾
Stylus Pressure: ☐ Color ☐ Pressure

the window, and paint to smooth out the high contrast reflections (Figure 2.57).

10. Select **Image: Adjust: Curves**. Modify the RGB composite curve with 1 point, making the input/output values read **118: 200**. This will lighten the entire window, making it appear illuminated.

11. Invert the selection by choosing **Invert** from the Select menu. Switch to Quick Mask and modify the selection so that only the facade on the front left of the image is selected (Figure 2.58).

12. Select **Image: Adjust: Color Balance**, and click the **Shadows** radio button. Set the sliders to cyan/red -17, magenta/green +86, and yellow/blue +25 (Figure 2.59). This emulates the cold green cast typical of most outdoor fluorescent lighting.

13. Invert the selection again and modify the color to reflect the compliment of the light casting the shadow. In this case, the light source is green, so the shadows should tint magenta. Select **Image: Adjust: Curves**. Modify the Green curve with 2 points, making the input/output values read **168: 200, 29: 17**. Modify the

LIBRARIE EMOM @ 26.9% (RGB)

26.86% | Doc: 8.55M/10.5M

Figure 2.60 *Pushing magenta into the shadows with the Curves command.*

LIBRARIE EMOM @ 26.9% (Quick Mask)

Figure 2.58 *Quick Mask selection of the left storefronts.*

Info | Options | Brushes

35 45 65 100 400

26.86% | Doc: 8.55M/12.0M

RECIPE: — CONTINUED

Figure 2.61 *The final image.*

Blue curve with 2 points as well, making the input/output values read **194: 143, 65: 62** (Figure 2.60).

14. Choose the Polygon Lasso tool and select the ground outside the shop window, avoiding the foreground objects and the vertical sections of the step beside the building.

15. Select the Airbrush and **Option**-click to sample the light blue color in the shop window. Lightly paint the light cascading out of the shop.

Finishing the image entailed pushing and pulling contrasts and colors until the effect pulls together. The green facade was selected independently of the shop windows, and the contrast was stretched to restate the darks. In addition, more magenta was pushed into the shadows by dodging and burning in just the green channel. Figure 2.61 shows the final image.

Chapter 3

UNDERSTANDING DIGITAL COLOR

At work in the painting studio, the last thing an artist would think about would be complicated color models, values, and gamuts. If someone were to impose the complicated color restrictions that exist in the digital world to the studio, they would be laughed out the door. Color was once as simple as squeezing out a bit of cerulean blue, adding some rose madder, a little paynes gray, some white, and there you go. The great thing about mixing color in the painting studio was that you could absolutely trust your eyes … if it looked good, it *was* good.

There are two areas that impact working with color in Photoshop: variation between devices and the contrasting gamuts of color models. At this point, some of you are muttering that digital color is a big pain, and that the last thing you want to learn is a bunch of numbers and charts that represent the glow in a girl's cheeks. Although we all may pine for the days of mixing color on a paint palette, the reality of digital color is that it needs to be managed from scan to print. It's an integral component of digital design, and ignoring it is like avoiding the harder scales of a musical instrument, hoping you will never have to play in that key.

The reality of digital color is that it needs to be managed from scan to print.

Device Variation

If you lined up tubes of cerulean blue oil paint from all the major manufacturers: Grumbacher, Windsor Newton, Talons et al., and compared the colors, you would see a tremendous variation. One manufacturer uses more binder, another more pigment, another, purer pigment materials. The result is many tubes of color, sharing the same name but looking very different. In the studio, you simply use the hue you like best and make adjustments in the mixing stage.

Until recently, manufacturers in the computer industry were doing the same thing as paint manufacturers. The red on one printer does not look the same as it does on another. The reasons vary from quality of the paper used to software programming, but the end result is the same as with the oil paint.

The act of digitizing color information necessitates that all computers, printers, and scanners know what we mean by cerulean blue. Otherwise, each time the same piece is printed or viewed on a different computer, the look is going to change dramatically. If the same painting changed color each time you looked at it, you would be just as concerned about oils as you are about your digital image.

In the world of oil painting, there is no compelling reason for all the paint manufacturers to bring their cerulean blues into spectral consistency. In the digital world, there is an obviously compelling reason, as no one will take digital imaging seriously if there is no efficient way to handle color. After a few false starts from various manufacturers who lacked the technology or the marketing push, Apple has emerged as the color management leader with its ColorSync system.

The ColorSync system uses device profiles that define how a monitor, scanner, or printer looks at color. Once the profile is established, the ColorSync engine works in the background, compensating for the varying points of view of the different devices. There's not a lot more you need to know other than to be sure you have profiles for the various components in your system and that you use them.

At the system level, you can select the ColorSync profile by opening the ColorSync Profile control panel and selecting the profile that

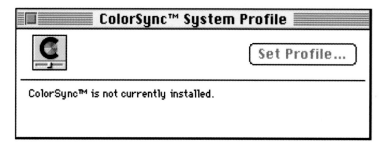

Figure 3.1 *The ColorSync control panel allows full control over various device targets and profiles.*

most closely matches your display (Figure 3.1). At the Photoshop preferences level, configure the Monitor Set-up command as described in Chapter 1. When applicable, the ColorSync profiles for your scanner and printer will be selectable from the various print setup screens and scanner interfaces.

Managing color across devices is not a perfect science. The way your computer's processor looks at color is much more of an exact science. The more you understand, the more intuitively you will be able to work with color in your images.

The Color Models and Their Gamuts

Digital images use different color models in describing a color. You will hear the terms RGB and CMYK quite a bit, along with more theoretical color spaces like HSV, HSB, HSL (all the same space, by the way), YCC, LAB, LUV, and more. These models are referred to as "spaces" in that the way they describe a range of color that can be defined and graphed. The range of colors that can be described by a certain space is called its gamut. When a color space cannot describe a certain color, that color is said to be "out of gamut."

RECIPE: — COLOR CAST REMOVAL

It's hard to give a global method for color correcting images, given that each image can have a wide range of subject matter, lighting conditions, and intended uses. Therefore, the most important skill is to understand the process behind making effective color corrections.

Good color corrections emphasize the important areas of an image, while minimizing areas that might distract. The example used here is a renaissance drawing by Raphael, taken from a stock photo collection. The image is in Photo-CD format and is a good illustration of many of the issues you may face while correcting color.

The main challenge is that the camera does not understand that the marks on the paper are far more important than the paper itself. Therefore, it picks up the folds, wrinkles, and highlights of the paper. The goal will be to color correct so as to articulate the drawing itself, minimizing the physical details in the paper (Figure 3.2).

Rather than setting the white or black point, which would serve to emphasize the shadows in the paper, the first goal is to neutralize the paper color itself. If the paper carries no distracting color cast, emphasizing the drawing becomes easier. The RGB values for the paper were estimated to be within ten points of each other for it to read as neutral.

Figure 3.2 The initial photo of the Raphael drawing.

Sample values of the paper were taken by moving the cursor into the desired position in the image and taking readings in the Get Info palette. Careful attention was given to where the sampling was taken, choosing one that would be easy to replicate with multiple samplings.

1. Begin by lowering the red curve, with the intention of getting even values across the RGB settings. Select **Image: Adjust: Curves** and choose only the red channel from the Channel pop-up menu. Here we've brought the red setting from 199 to 183, more in line with the median blue setting of 179 (Figure 3.3).
2. The next step is to raise the green values up towards the median blue value. Select **Image: Adjust: Curves** again, this time selecting the green channel from the Channel pop-up menu. In this example, they were adjusted from 160 to 164 (Figure 3.4).

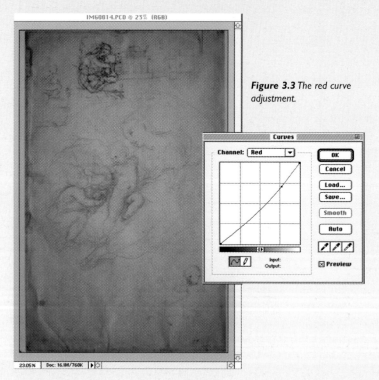

Figure 3.3 The red curve adjustment.

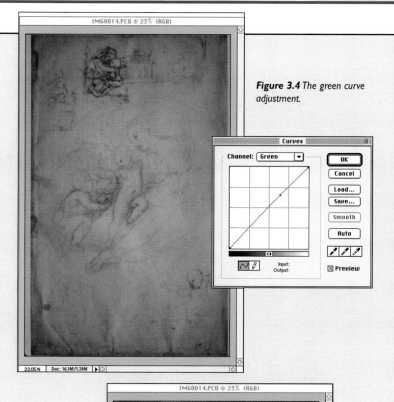

Figure 3.4 *The green curve adjustment.*

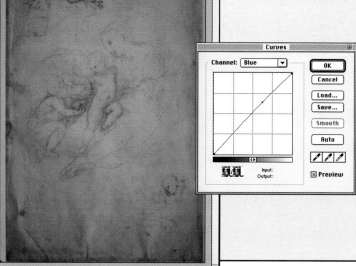

Figure 3.5 *The blue curve adjustment.*

3. A final color tweak is given to the blue curve, raising it slightly from 163 to 168 (Figure 3.5). This final color range of 165G to 175R gives a slightly warm color cast, which seems appropriate with this sort of renaissance image.

4. A final S-curve adjustment is given to emphasize and create contrast in the midtones, making the drawing more visible (Figure 3.6).

5. As a final step, the curve configuration is saved to be loaded the next time a Photo-CD image of a drawing needs to be corrected. To do this, select **Save** from the Curves dialog box, name the curve and save it to a place where you can find it when you need it. To access it, select **Load** and choose the file (Figure 3.7).

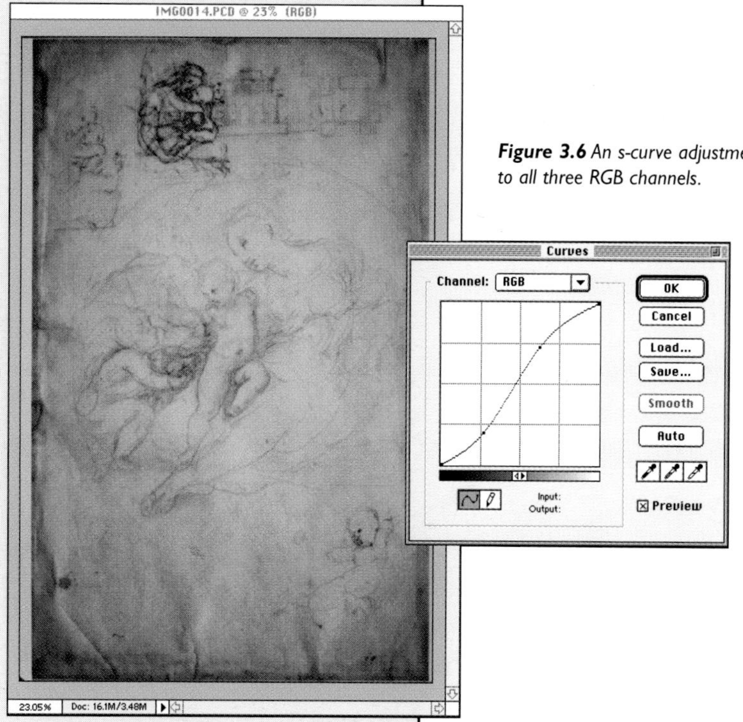

Figure 3.6 *An s-curve adjustment to all three RGB channels.*

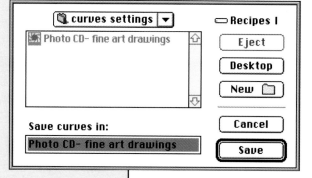

Figure 3.7 *The Save Curve Settings dialog box.*

54

RGB and Indexed—Color for the Screen

RGB—which stands for red, green, and blue—is the native color space of the digital medium. The monitor you look at uses red, green, and blue pixels to describe every color on your screen, and most scanners capture their images through red, green, and blue filters. Figure 3.8 shows the RGB color space.

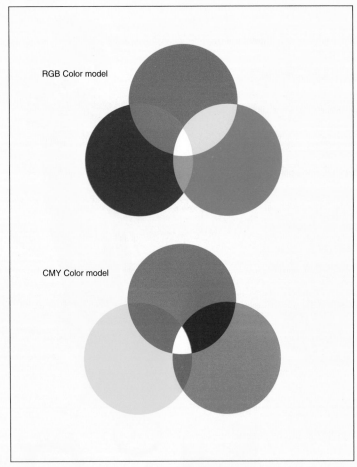

Figure 3.8 *The digital color palette is based on the RGB color space. The inverse of RGB is CMY.*

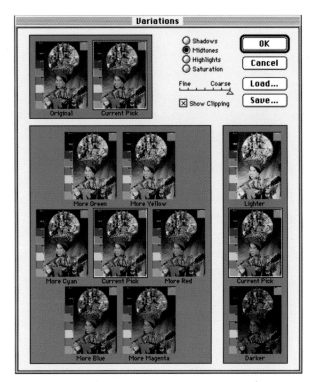

Figure 3.9 *The Variations dialog box is a good way to visualize color relationships.*

If only we could print in the RGB format, the circle from capture to modification to printing would be complete. Unfortunately, this will never happen because RGB is a luminous color space, in that the light is passed through an object from behind, registering on receptors in front of the device. The monitor shoots white light through the screen to be received by your eyes. The scanner shoots the light through filters to be received by the CCD or PMT sensors. Other examples of luminous devices are your television, stained glass windows, and one of my favorite toys of all time, the Lite Brite. As we will see, the CMYK space is reflective, which is why we must jump through hoops when we take a digital image to print.

RGB is an additive color space. Adding 100% of all three colors equals white. Each color of RGB is represented by a grayscale image

Intuitive Color Inversion

It is extremely important to understand the inverse relationship between RGB and CMYK color spaces. When you add red to an image, you automatically subtract its inverse, which is cyan. The other color pairs are green/magenta and yellow/blue.

It is important to develop a feel for the color relationships by experimenting and gathering information before learning the numbers. In fact, it can be pretty confusing to look at the info palette and see that the RGB/CMYK values for the same color look very different. CMYK's tendency to show the color values as percentages of the total plate value does not match RGB's 0–255 value range.

A good way to visualize the color relationships is to go to the Variations command in the Adjust submenu in the Image menu (Figure 3.9). The Variations dialog box allows you to look at a thumbnail of your current image, surrounded by a color wheel of thumbnails. Each color wheel thumbnail takes the image in the direction of the color that bears its name. Move the slider in the upper right from Fine to Coarse to see these color relationships exaggerated.

In this dialog box, it is easy to see how the inverse relationships play against each other. Don't just look at the overall color casts. Pay attention at this point to a patch of orange or the green of a tree. What happens to orange when you add cyan? What happens when you take green away from the tree? Does it get less green, more magenta, or brown as a color should when you add its compliment?

Work with these relationships until you get a solid feel for the relationship between colors. Remember that you very seldom use a color that is at 100% intensity, which means it plays between the polarities we're discussing. Learn to push and pull these polarities until you achieve the perfect shade.

(Figure 3.10 A–D), which shows the relative value of each pixel for that color. For example, if a certain pixel had RGB values of 112R, 68G, and 198B, the green channel would represent that pixel with a gray value of 68. The two things to understand from the three RGB values is that higher numbers mean more color is present, and that the relationship and balance between the colors determines what a color looks like. Remember that all of the colors at 100% (255) equal white. This implies that they cancel each other out if they are equal across the board.

Open the Channels palette and click on each channel separately, looking at them one at a time. The darker the grayscale tones, the less of that particular color is in the image. A lighter grayscale tone indi-

Figures 3.10 A–D
The RGB model creates a separate grayscale plate for each color.

cates more of that color in the image (Figures 3.11 A, B). Imagine the luminous nature of RGB as you try to picture this. Visualize the green being projected through the channel to make up the image. The darker tones block the green light from getting through, allowing its opposite (magenta) to appear. Lighter grayscale tones allow more of the color to pass through and appear in the image. Although this isn't what really happens, it can help you visualize and interpret how a grayscale channel impacts the look of the overall image.

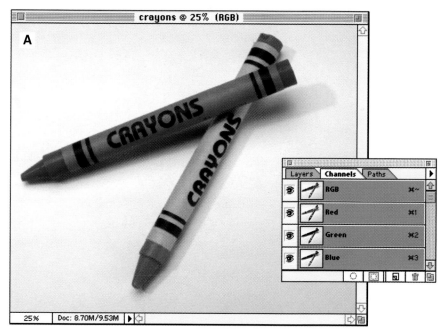

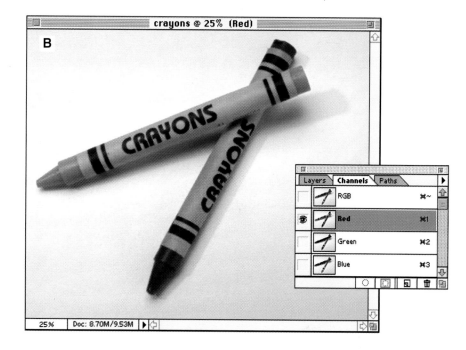

Figures 3.11 A, B *An RGB channel shows areas of high color concentration as lighter tones. A shows the red channel; B shows the composite image.*

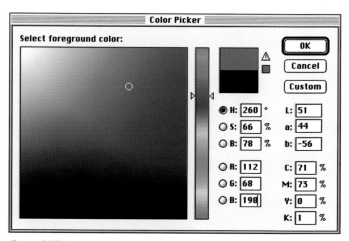

Figure 3.12 *Learn to anticipate color results from a set of numbers.*

Examining on the local level means looking at pixel values. The color described by 112R, 68G, 198B is a bluish purple, which you can tell by the high blue number, median red number, and low green number (Figure 3.12). If two values are relatively close, the resulting color is usually the inverse of the low number. Bring the red up to 198, for example, and the color looks more magenta, which is the inverse of green. (See the sidebar on RGB/CMYK comparisons for more on inverse color relationships.)

The wide range of color that RGB describes makes it the perfect space for projects designed for on-screen viewing. This allows designers to create and show images in the same luminous space. Web designers, multimedia presenters, and video game designers all fall into this category.

RECIPE: — RGB CHANNEL DISTORTIONS

This recipe shows how the various channels interact to create a realistic image. It also shows how the channel relationships can be modified to create impressive abstract color effects.

The example shown here takes a single standalone object and abstracts the color space. While this same effect could be applied to a number of other image types, this one is the most illustrative.

1. Select the apple using the Magic Wand, Quick Mask, or any of Photoshop's other selection tools. Once selected, choose **Select: Save Selection** to save the selection to a separate channel (Figure 3.13).

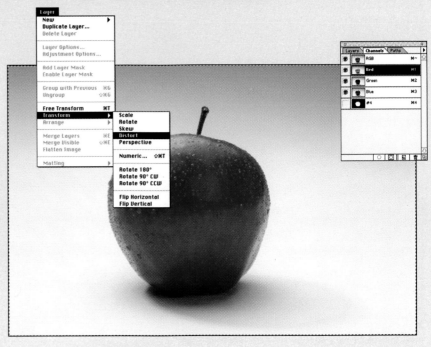

Figure 3.14 With the Red channel active and all channels visible, select **Distort** from the Transform submenu

2. Open the Channels palette and click on **Red** to highlight the Red channel, while clicking the visibility icon in the RGB icon. This will highlight the Red channel as the channel to be modified, while allowing you to view the entire image.

3. Choose **Select: Select All** to select the entire image, then select **Layer: Transform: Distort** (Figure 3.14). This will create handles at the corners of the image, which are dragged to apply the distortion. Drag the handles, keeping in mind that they can be dragged outside of the image window to stretch the image . In this case, the major distortion is to the left. (Figure 3.15). Once the distortion is in place, click on the **Move** tool, and click **Apply** to accept the distortion.

Figure 3.13 Select the object and save it to a separate channel.

Figure 3.15 *Drag the handles to view the distortion of the red channel.*

Figure 3.16 *Using the Airbrush, feather the hard edges around the red channel distortion.*

4. In the Channels palette, deselect the Visibility icon in all channels except the Red channel, which will show the Red channel as a grayscale image. Choose **Select: None**, set the foreground color to white, and select the Airbrush. Using a large feathered brush, soften and feather the hard edges around the distortion area (Figure 3.16).

5. In the Channels palette, reset the Visibility icon to the RGB channel, bringing the entire image back into view. Click on the Green

RECIPE: — CONTINUED

Figure 3.18 *Using the Airbrush, feather the hard edges around the Green channel distortion.*

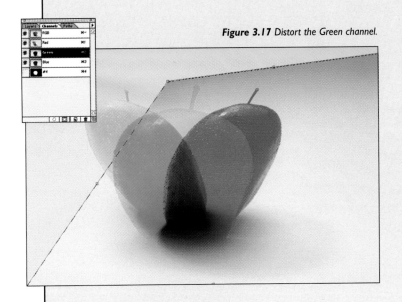

Figure 3.17 *Distort the Green channel.*

channel to highlight it as the channel to be modified, Select **All** from the Select menu, then **Layer: Transform: Distort**. Drag the handles to distort the Green channel, and apply the changes as before (Figure 3.17).

6. In the Channels palette, activate the visibility icon only in the Green channel, which will show the green channel as a grayscale image. Set the foreground color to white and select the Airbrush.

Using a large feathered brush, soften and feather the hard edges around the distortion area (Figure 3.18).

7. Repeat the distortion process for the Blue channel, selecting the channel, distorting it, and cleaning up the edges of the distortion (Figure 3.19). The result will be an image that stretches the object in opposite directions. This shows the way colors interact and how their combinations result in various hues (Figure 3.20).

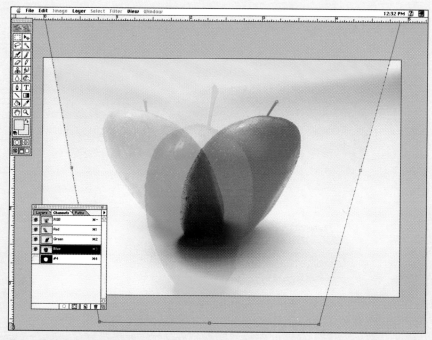

Figure 3.19 Distort tne Blue channel and clean up the edges.

Figure 3.20 The composite image, showing the interaction of the three channels.

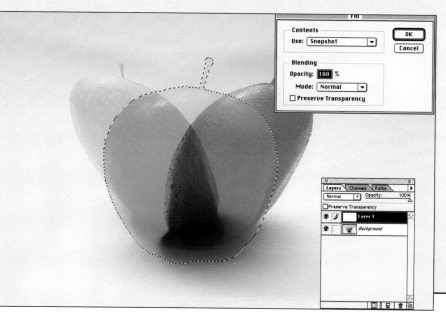

8. Create a new layer and load the selection you saved in step 1 by selecting **Load Selection** from the Select menu.

9. With the new layer active, choose **Edit: Fill** and select **Snapshot** in the Use pop-up menu in the Contents section. Leave Opacity at 100% and the Mode at Normal (Figure 3.21). Click **OK** to fill the original apple image into the selection in the new layer.

Figure 3.21 Fill the new layer selection from the snapshot image.

RECIPE: — CONTINUED

10. With the image reloaded on a separate layer, experiment with the various apply modes in the pop-up menu of the Layers palette. In this case, **Hard Light** was selected, with Opacity left at 100% (Figure 3.22). While you could have made these changes in step 9 in the fill dialog box, this method gives you more flexibility.

11. With the apple still selected, create a third layer. Double-click the Rubber Stamp tool to open the Rubber Stamp Options palette, selecting **From Snapshot** in the Option pop-up menu. Vary the opacity and paint in the top of the apple, making it blend with the layers below (Figure 3.23). The final image has been sharpened a bit in the top layer, especially around the stem and the water droplets (Figure 3.24).

Figure 3.23 Use the Rubber Stamp to paint the top of the apple in from the snapshot.

Figure 3.22 Using the Hard Light apply mode.

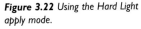

Figure 3.24
The final image.

Indexed as an Option

In RGB, each 8-bit color channel creates 256 shades of gray so that it can vary its intensity and value. Another option for on-screen solutions is to convert your image to indexed color, which maps all of the colors in your image into a look-up table referenced by the file. This color look-up table (CLUT) can contain up to 256 colors (Figure 3.25).

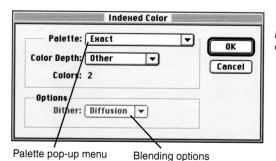

Palette pop-up menu   Blending options

Figure 3.26 The Indexed Color dialog box.

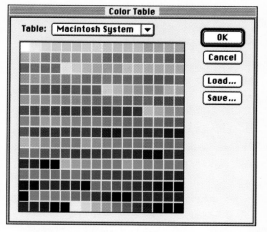

Figure 3.25 The default Color Look-Up Table (CLUT) as shown on the Macintosh system.

While this sounds like a small amount compared to the 16 million colors available in 24-bit RGB, Indexed color does a great job for on-screen viewing. Converting a wide range of colors down to 256 options does call for sacrifices, especially in the shadow areas. Indexed color, though, received a real shot in the arm with the growing popularity of Web graphics. Web designers, along with the video game and presentation designers, can take full advantage of indexed color's smaller file size while maintaining most of its image quality.

Most conversions to indexed color use adaptive palette for the palette option, and this is the mode that you should use for most of the work you do. There are more options under the Palette pop-up menu, most of which are self-explanatory (Figure 3.26). The Exact option converts the image to indexed color using the exact colors that appear in your image. This obviously places a limitation of 256 colors on your original image. If your original image has more than 256 colors, this option is grayed out. The System Mac and Windows palettes convert the image using the closest color match from each system's

default color tables. The Web palette most closely matches the default palettes of Web browsers. The Uniform palette takes a regular sampling of the entire color spectrum, giving a balanced cross section of colors available. For 8-bit color depth, Photoshop takes six evenly spaced color samples of red, green, and blue and calculates the combination to produce 216 colors.

The Custom palette allows you to specify the exact colors you want to use to translate your image. Clicking **Custom** brings up the default color palette for your system, allowing you to click on individual colors and modify them as you wish. A quick way of getting custom results is to select an area of the image before you convert to indexed color. Photoshop automatically weights the color conversion toward any active selection. This means that if you select a grassy area before converting, the CLUT will have a stronger concentration of green tones, reflecting what was in the selection. In this way, you can select areas of importance, which should carry extra emphasis and color detail.

Because an indexed color image has a narrow range of color to choose from, it has to be ingenious in how it handles the transitions from one color to another. The blending options that appear in the Dither pop-up menu of the Index Color dialog box are Diffusion, Pattern, and None (Figure 3.27). By selecting **None**, you apply no blending between colors at all, which posterizes the image into areas of flat color. The Diffusion option is the best for blending, and it is in fact the only option for all of the Palette options except for the System (Macintosh) palette. The Diffusion option creates a random speckled

Figure 3.27 The dithering options for indexed color conversions.

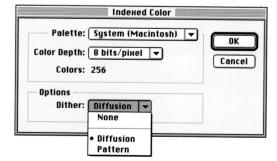

effect that helps create a smoother transition between colors. The Pattern option, in case you're curious, creates an ugly pattern of dots, making your image look as through it was printed on an old 9-pin dot matrix printer. Since it's only available when the Macintosh System Palette is selected, Adobe probably had the Apple Imagewriter in mind as they created it. That does not keep Windows users from selecting the Mac palette and printing to any dot matrix printer, if they should be so inclined.

Color for Print—CMYK

Because most computer-generated images are not viewed on the computer, we are forced to deal with CMYK as a color space. Cyan, magenta, yellow, and black are the color variables in this space, and the very nature of the variables indicate that the CMYK space is different from the other spaces discussed.

Except for CMYK, all color spaces use what is called a trichromatic approach, using three variables such as RGB, LAB, or YCC. This is because three variables deliver the widest gamut with the least amount of overhead. The CMYK model uses the same trichromatic approach, given that CMY is the exact inverse of RGB. The problem is that CMY does not work the way it is supposed to, so we have to add a black plate to even things out.

The main reason for CMY's failure to pull its own weight is that it is *reflective* rather than *luminous* (light is bounced off the page rather than shining through it). This is problematic for the following reasons:

- Light sources can vary in intensity and color, changing the look of the printed piece. Your monitor and scanner always use the same light source, so the results can be calibrated to look the same every time.
- Printing inks contain impurities that compromise the possible range of color combinations. This is why the maximum ink densities of cyan, magenta, and yellow give a brownish gray rather than black.
- Printed pieces in CMYK are compromised by glare from the page reflecting back to the viewer. Luminous devices such as monitors bounce the glare back toward the light source, rather than out to the viewer. If your monitor gives you glare, lower the room light and adjust the angle away from any windows.

- Because CMYK is a subtractive medium, in which the absence of all color is white, it stands to reason that the whitest areas of the printed piece are limited to the whiteness of the paper. This can vary depending on job lots and it is very difficult to simulate on your computer screen.
- The way the ink is applied to the paper varies from day to day, depending on the relative humidity, the guy running the press, and other local factors.

The result is a system in which black prints brown, the overall color gamut is dramatically reduced, and the ink is absorbed into the paper, blurring the results. Unfortunately, CMYK is the color space we must work in if we are going to produce a printed piece.

HOW TO LOOK AT A CMYK IMAGE

The CMYK values in an image are broken into four channels instead of the three that we saw with RGB. A big difference from RGB is that the CMYK channels are measured as percentages ranging from 1% to 100%. A 100% value would be a full-sized dot of the ink on the paper, as determined by the screen size. A 5% value would literally be a dot that's 5% of the full-sized dot (Figure 3.28). The amount of CMYK data is the opposite of the RGB, given that a low RGB number signifies a dark tone (absence of light), while a higher CMYK percentage equals the same dark tone (presence of ink).

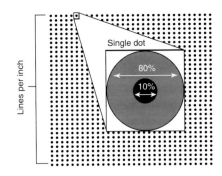

Figure 3.28 *The DPI determines the size of each cell in the grid, while the dot percentage refers to the percentage of each cell filled in.*

The Secondary Color Spaces

RGB and CMYK are considered to be the primary color spaces, given that all images must be converted to one of these spaces for nearly all applications. The secondary spaces have some value in the intermediate stages, although it is probably more important to be aware of them than to master them.

LAB COLOR

LAB color has been heralded as the perfect intermediate color space, since it theoretically contains all of the values of perceptible color. Because it has such a wide gamut, it is the perfect space to use as a central point when converting from one color to another. It understands all of the various color spaces and knows how to translate the values from one space to another. LAB is central to most color-management software and it is Photoshop's native color space.

Rather than looking at an image as having a separate color for each channel, LAB divides the image into one channel for the tonal characteristics and uses the other two channels to describe polarities between two opposing colors (Figure 3.29).

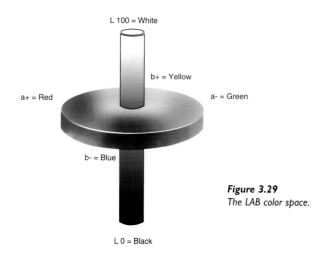

Figure 3.29
The LAB color space.

The L channel in LAB refers to the luminance in the image, which is dictated by the lights and darks. This channel can make tonal changes without affecting the color balance of the image, which is

very useful. The A channel describes the color balance between green and magenta, and the B channel shows the balance between blue and yellow. If you find concept of balance confusing, remember that the red channel in the RGB model is actually the balance between red and cyan. Lowering the red value actually adds cyan to the image. The same is true for green and magenta, and yellow and blue. LAB is able to focus more on the balancing aspects since it exists as more of a theoretical space.

HSL, HSV, AND SOMETIMES HSB

For some reason, the color space referred to in Photoshop as HSL is also known as HSV and HSB. *HSL* stands for hue, saturation, and lightness, with the *L* being replaced by *V* for value, and *B* for brightness. They all mean the same thing. The HSL model actually comes closest to the way we mix colors in a painting studio, and, for that reason, many artists find it easier to use.

The Hue value refers to the general color family, such as blue or green. The numbers in this value are actually numeric places around the color wheel, measured in degrees. The easiest way to see how numbers represent colors is to open the Photoshop Color palette and type in degree settings and watch the numbers change. If you prefer, you can change the color picker to the Apple and view the actual color wheel and the relative color positions (Figure 3.30). To do this, select **General Preferences** in the File menu, and select **Apple** from the Color Picker pop-up menu. Then click on the foreground color swatch to look at the color wheel.

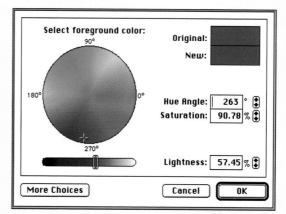

Figure 3.30 *The Apple Color Picker is based on the HSL color space.*

The saturation value refers to the purity of the color. This can also be looked at as how a color is tinted. A low saturation value is a color with a lot of white mixed in, while a high saturation is more pure color. Lightness refers to the brightness of the color, which reflects the amount of black mixed into the color. Again, a low lightness value is a blackened color, while a high value is more of the pure color. The HSL model is the closest thing to mixing paint in the studio, both in process and results.

OTHER SECONDARY SPACES

There are other color spaces out there that you may stumble across from time to time. Kodak has its YCC space that it uses for Photo-CD, there are the CIE XYZ and CIE LUV spaces that were the pre-cursors to the LAB model we use today, and probably a few others. The point is that we are trying to wrap our arms around color so we can work intuitively. If you master RGB and CMYK, you will be in great shape. If the LAB or HSL models are helpful, use them as well.

How to Manipulate Color

Obviously there is more to workflow than just knowing how color is organized. The big question is how do you effectively and easily modify the color in your image. Photoshop offers more ways to modify color and you can decide for yourself if one way is better than another for your specific needs. Having said that, there is one color control that must be mastered if you want to intuitively work with Photoshop: the Curves control.

The Numbers of Digital Color

Given digital color's reliance numbers, it can be confusing to keep all of the numbers straight. The following list illustrates how all the numbers interact.

- Number 1: One pixel. All digital values are applied to one pixel at a time.
- Number 3: Tri-chromatic. All color spaces except CMYK use three color variables to mix color values. RGB, HSL, LAB, and even CMY all measure values through a color channel.
- Number 8: 8 bits per channel. Each pixel is given 8 bits of data to describe the intensity of each color variable. This 2^8 power value results in 256 tones or values to express each color variable's intensity. This is why each color channel is described with a 256-level grayscale image.
- Number 24: 24-bit color. The combination of three 8-bit variables (RGB, LAB, etc.) results in 16,777,216 color combinations.
- Number 32: 32-bit color. Because CMYK has four 8-bit variables, it has a 32-bit color space. In theory, this would give it 4,294,967,296 different colors to choose from. As mentioned previously, the limitations of the printing system dramatically reduces this number.
- Number 16: 16 bits per channel. Each pixel is given 16 bits of data to describe the intensity of each color variable. This 2^{16} power value results in 32,768 tones or values to express each color channel. This process is not supported by most software applications today and is useful only in scanning a wide range of data that gets reduced when it is brought into Photoshop.
- Number 48: 48-bit color. The combination of three 16-bit variables (RGB, LAB, etc.) results in way too many color combinations. As mentioned previously, this space has limited uses and is not supported significantly by most software packages.

Color Modifiers: Where and When to Use Them

All of the many color modifiers in Photoshop are listed next with a brief explanation of where they work best.

- Brightness/Contrast. Two sliders adjust the brightness and contrast. Without much control over the image or the adjustments, it's a down and dirty control option.
- Levels. Three triangle sliders compress the shadows, midtones, and highlights in a histogram. It uses the RGB 0 to 255 value scale, setting the midpoint at 100 (1.0). The Levels command also adjusts the white and black inputs with a slider. Good for evaluating histograms and setting basic white point, it's also good in that it uses actual RGB values rather than an arbitrary -100 to +100 numeric range, and it allows modification of individual color channels.
- Curves. It plots tonal range over the entire range for composite image or individual channels. Curves gives all image data in both RGB or CMYK percentages and allows modification of individual color channels. The section on curves later in this chapter goes into extensive detail on this feature.
- Color Balance. This control allows subtle tweaks of color casts in highlights, midtones, or shadows. A great fine-tuning tool, it isolates the highlights, shadows, and mids as the changes are made.
- Hue/Saturation. It gives HSL controls over an RGB/CMYK image, allowing you to change hue, intensity, or lightness, and to colorize the entire image.
- Desaturate. With no controls on this one, select it and it removes all color from an image, reducing it to grayscale.
- Replace Color. A fancy hue/saturation control, this feature lets you isolate a color and use HSL sliders to change it.
- Selective Color. This feature selects specific color components in the image and lets you modify them with RGB or CMYK color sliders.
- Invert. Select this no-dialog command to create a negative of your image, inverting tonality as well as hue.
- Equalize. It redistributes the brightness values in the image across the available tonal range image. There is no dialog here either, just click and go.
- Threshold. This control converts images to black and white, with a slider to determine threshold point of what's black and what's white.
- Posterize. Selecting this feature specifies the number of tonal levels in the image, creating a solarized effect.
- Variations. It displays visual thumbnails of the image along with color variations arranged in a color wheel. This is a purely visual point-and-click interface to choose what corrections you're after.

RECIPE: — DUOTONE EFFECTS WITH SELECTIVE COLOR

Duotones are all the rage these days. The traditional method of combining a black plate with a plate of another color and achieving a tinted monochrome image, has really caught on in design circles. Duotones not only have a great patina and graphic feel, they also allow a much wider tonal range than a traditional black-and-white image. Sepia prints, cyanotypes, and other forms of nonsilver photo methods have also become popular, as designers are looking to present an alternative to a straightforward color or black-and-white image.

Photoshop does allow users to create duotones by selecting **Image: Mode: Duotone**, selecting two colors, and tweaking curves to control how the two colors interact in the image. This is a great approach for someone who really knows printing curves as they relate to tonal ranges and printing

Figure 3.32 Adjusting color cast in the shadows.

Figure 3.31 The original grayscale image.

press tolerances. Unfortunately, that does not include too many designers. The recipe that follows shows how to assimilate the look and extended range of some of these alternative processes while working in the familiar RGB color space. This method also allows you to add additional colors to produce tritone and quadtone effects, while applying the color exactly where you want it. Pay attention to how the added color increases the depth and range of the image, rather than simply responding to the color as a patina or graphic element.

1. Begin with a black-and-white image. If you are starting with a grayscale image, convert it to RGB by selecting **Image: Mode: RGB Color**. If your image is RGB already, select **Image: Mode: Grayscale** clicking **Yes** to discard color information. Once in grayscale, select **Image: Mode: RGB Color** to change the mode back to RGB. Figure 3.31 shows my original image.

2. Select **Image: Adjust: Selective Color** to bring up the Selective Color dialog box. With the Relative and Preview options checked, choose **Blacks** from the Colors pop-up menu, and adjust the color sliders to add a color cast only to the dark areas of the image. In this example, a yellow/red cast was added to the shadows (Figure 3.32). Do not click OK after adjusting the sliders.

3. While still in the Selective Color dialog box, choose **Neutrals** from the pop-up menu and push a color cast into the neutral areas of the image. For most images, this will impact the overall look more than anything else. In this case, more magenta was removed, which pushed a strong green cast into the image. Small amounts of red and yellow were also added to achieve the right balance (Figure 3.33). Do not click OK after making these adjustments.

4. While still in the Selective Color dialog box, choose **Whites** from the pop-up menu, and push a color cast into the highlight areas of the image. This is the narrowest range of color for most images and is useful for enhancing effects already applied. One exception is the black slider. Reducing the black slider in the Whites section can stretch the tonal range, allowing more definition in the highlight areas. In this case, large amounts of green and red were added to the highlights, and the black plate was reduced (Figure 3.34). At this point you may choose to fine-tune the color balance, moving through the Blacks, Neutrals, and Whites sections, making changes as you go. When the color is right, click **OK** to apply the changes.

5. Select **Edit: Take Snapshot** to save a copy of the current image to the snapshot area (Figure 3.35).

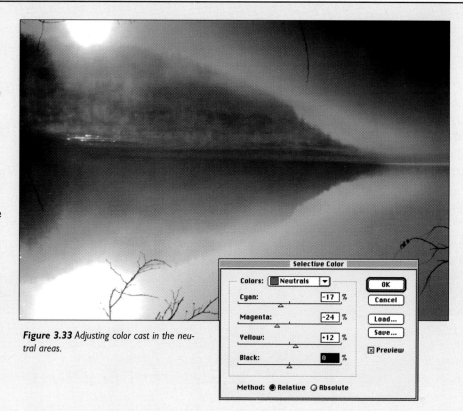

Figure 3.33 *Adjusting color cast in the neutral areas.*

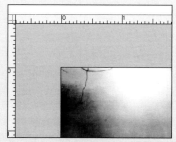

Figure 3.34 *Adjusting the color cast in the highlights.*

Figure 3.35
*Select **Take Snapshot**.*

RECIPE: — CONTINUED

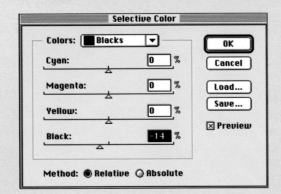

Figure 3.36 Reopen Selective Color and lighten the Black slider in the Blacks color area.

6. To add even more range to the image, select **Image: Adjust: Selective Color**, selecting the **Blacks** option in the Colors pop-up menu. Lower the Black slider, which lightens the overall image, widening the range in the lighter areas (Figure 3.36).

7. To replace the darks that were lost in step 6, double-click the Rubber Stamp tool to access the Rubber Stamp Options palette. Set the Option menu to **From Snapshot,** and the Apply Mode at **Normal.** Varying the opacity and brush size, paint the dark areas back in.

8. In this example, two views were used to see the entire image, as well as the detailed areas that were being modified. To open an additional view, select **View: New View** and scroll/zoom as needed. With multiple views open, the changes made to one window are automatically reflected in all the other views. This allows detailed changes to be made in the branches while keeping an eye on the overall image (Figure 3.37). In the final image, the colors work on a graphic level without getting in the way of the overall tonal range (Figure 3.38).

Figure 3.38 The final image.

Figure 3.37 With multiple views open, paint back the darks with the Rubber Stamp tool.

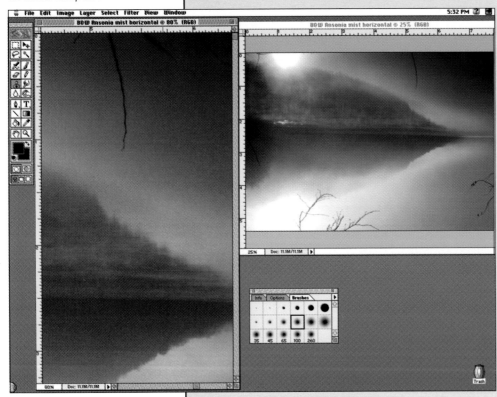

Why Curves Are So Important

Curves pack more control into a single dialog box than any other Photoshop command. They allow global or local changes to be executed with pinpoint accuracy. You could take away all other Photoshop color controls except for curves and still retain most of Photoshop's color capabilities.

Curves allow you to increase or decrease color and tonal saturation, either to the entire image or within each individual channel. You can make subtle color variations, or you can completely abstract the color relationships within the piece. While there may be other components within Photoshop that can be used for controlling color, none is as singularly useful as curves.

ANATOMY OF A CURVE

The main Curves control is a grid of five intersecting lines horizontally and vertically. These lines represent the tonal areas in the image: highlights, 1/4 tones, midtones, 3/4 tones, and blacks (Figure 3.39). It is also possible to **Option**-click on the grid to enlarge it, which allows finer control over the tonal range in the image.

The actual tonal range in your image is represented by a diagonal line running from the lower left to the upper right. Understand that a curve is not a histogram, as it does not change its shape based on the actual data in your image. It is a representation of the tonal range, from darkest to lightest. You could click on the 3/4 tone area of the curve and tweak it up to the highlights and your image will not change if there is no data in the 3/4 tone area.

Exactly what that diagonal line represents is determined by the Channel pop-up menu and the tone direction arrows (Figure 3.40). The Channel pop-up menu allows you to modify the curve of your

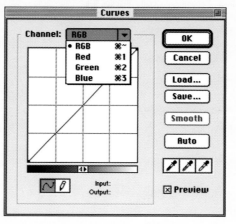

Figure 3.40 The Curves Channel pop-up menu.

entire image, or of each individual channel. Whether it's RGB, CMYK, or LAB, you can intensify or minimize each color channel separately. At the bottom of the Curves box there is a gradient going from black to white or white to black, with a set of double arrows in the middle. This tells you the tonal direction of your curve. The tone in the lower-left corner of your curve tells you what value is represented there. If you prefer to have the tone run the other way, click on the double arrows in the middle to reverse its direction.

The idea is that you can access a specific point in the tonal range and move it to another area in the grid, modifying the tonal values of the image. That means you can click on the midtones of an image and brighten them up by 10% with a simple drag. To determine exactly how you are modifying the curve, there is an input-output scale in the lower right of the curve dialog box. When you click and hold on the curve, the input box tells you the value of the point you started on, and as you drag, it tells you the value it will change to (Figure 3.41). This makes it easy to click on the 50% mark, and move it down until

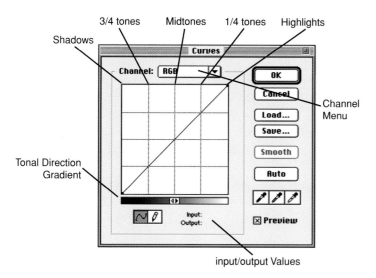

Figure 3.39 The curves dialog box.

it reads 42%. Be aware that the curve is dynamic. If you slide horizontally, you will move your input point as well as the output point.

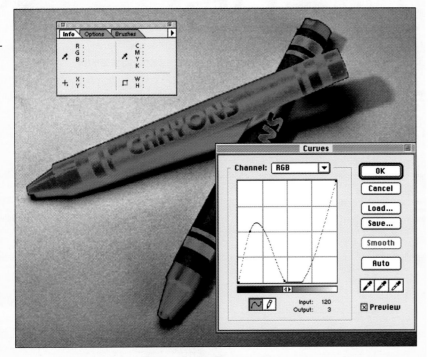

Figure 3.41 *You can modify specific values within the image, as determined by the shape of the curve.*

When in RGB, you can identify where a color falls on the curve by clicking on any color in the image itself. As you click and hold, a dot appears on the Composite RGB curve, showing you the position of that tone (Figure 3.42). You can even access individual channels through the Channels pop-up menu, and see how the selected point in the image relates to that one channel. Although you cannot apply this technique to the composite channel of a CMYK image, you can apply it to the individual CMYK channels.

CURVE BASICS

As you add points, you can dramatically change the look of your image. Anyone who has any practice with curves agrees that it is easy to abstract the color in the image, especially as you add multiple points in the curve. While you can use this to your advantage occa-

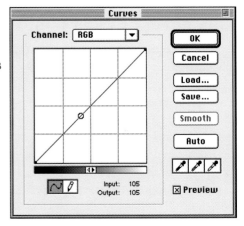

Figure 3.42 *Click on an RGB image pixel to see its corresponding placement on the curve.*

sionally, it has served to scare more people away from curves rather than endearing them. The main thing to remember is that the fewer the points and the smoother the curve, the more naturalistic the image (Figure 3.43). The abstract color changes come with more points and a bumpier curve.

One of the first things to do in the Curves dialog box is to set the white and black point of the image. This defines the outer limits of highlight and shadow detail in the image, while removing unwanted color casts. The point you click on is equalized to 0r0g0b for the black point, and 255r255g255b for the white point. In doing this, the tonal range between these points also shifts to a more neutral state, which often eliminates any unwanted color casts.

To set the white point, click on the White Point eyedropper in the lower right of the Curves dialog box, and move the cursor into the image itself. If you do not have the Info palette open and visible, cancel out of the Curves dialog box, open the Info palette and put it where you can see it. Circulate the Info palette around the lighter areas of your image, looking for the lightest area where you still want detail (Figure 3.44). Remember that any value greater than the white point you select will be reduced to flat white. If you selected a 25% gray tone, for example, all tones from 0% to 24% would be reduced to white. Again, you are looking for the lightest image area where you still want detail. Be careful also not to select a highlight that is too light. It is easy to go for the specular highlights, such as the reflections in chrome, or the flame of a candle, and set the white point there. This will have little effect on the overall image, in that these areas are

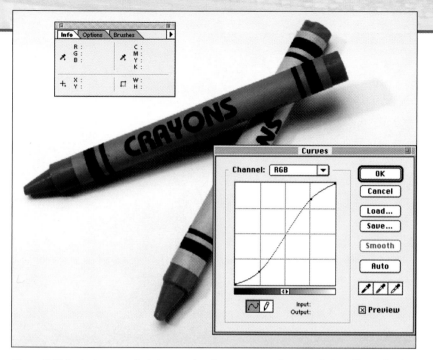

Figure 3.43 *As the image on the below reveals, color grows more abstract with the addition of multiple curve points. Though the image above has also been altered a great deal, it looks more naturalistic due to its smoother curve.*

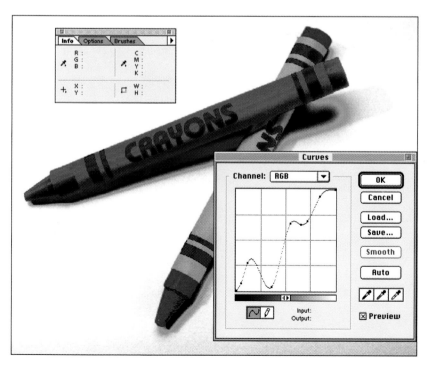

usually flat white to begin with. Go for the highlight area that has some detail but is not too dark.

Setting the black point follows the exact same principles, but in reverse. The Black Point eyedropper is the third from the right in the Curves dialog box, and it works the same as the White Point eyedropper. Find the darkest area where you still want detail and set your black point there. Once the endpoints of the curve are set, they do not change when the midpoints are moved. The only way to modify the white and black points further is to physically move the end points of the curve, or to use the white and black point eyedroppers.

A single point in the middle of a curve allows you to change all of the central points in the image, while keeping the ends stationary. If you wish to keep other areas of the image unaffected, anchor a point on the curve to hold the values in place. Be careful about doing this too much, or about modifying the curve too close to an anchor, as the normative color space can spin out of control.

Figure 3.44 *Avoiding the specular highlights; look for the lightest pixels in the image to set the white point.*

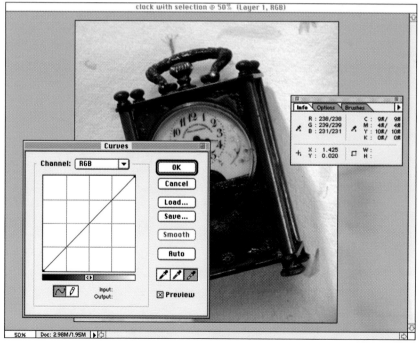

Lighter Highlights

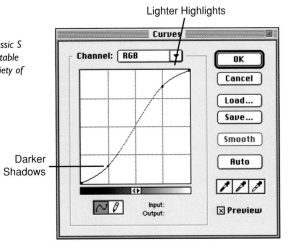

Figure 3.45 The classic S curve delivers predictable results in a wide variety of images

Darker Shadows

One of the most important things to remember about curves is that the basic shape of the curve effects the overall image. Specifically, the steeper areas of the curve reflect greater contrast, while the flatter areas reflect reduced contrast. Therefore, if you want to see more detail in the midtones of your image, you are forced to raise the highlights and perhaps lower the shadow areas (Figure 3.45). As you raise and lower these areas, please notice that the highlight to 1/4 tones and the 3/4 tones to shadow areas get flatter. Watch the image as you do this, and you will see the highlight and shadow detail flatten out, even as the overall contrast gets higher. This method of raising the highlights and lowering the shadows creates a classic S curve, which always delivers predictable results of increasing the contrast in the middle and punching up the darks.

Conclusion

It is important to understand how Photoshop starts with a bunch of numbers that somehow end up representing a wide gamut of subtle color possibilities. The digital medium forces us to take a cold, sometimes analytical approach to working with color, but this is the price we pay for repeatability and push-button accuracy.

Once you understand how Photoshop looks at color as values, you can quickly evaluate the relative strengths of an image based on its raw data. A solid evaluation of what values exist in an image will allow you to formulate a plan for bringing out specific areas or diminishing others. This ability to look at an image and understand how the values are distributed is a critical Photoshop skill.

Curves Shapes and their Results

While each image is unique in its correction requirements, some curves settings yield predictable results across similar images. Raising highlights or lowering midtones results in various curve shapes, to the point that a curve's results can be predicted by its shape. The standard S curve is a perfect example. The raised highlights and lowered shadows that form the S tend to stretch the color space in a predictable direction. A variety of curve shapes are listed next, accompanied by the resulting changes in the reference image.

- The S Curve. Raise the highlights and lower the shadows forming an S shape. This can punch the shadows and increase the contrast in a flat image. Overdoing it causes a loss of shadow detail, with stark tonal contrast.

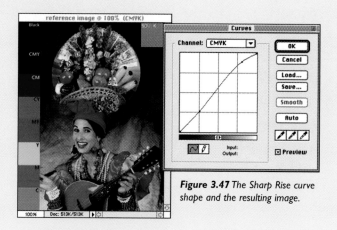

Figure 3.47 The Sharp Rise curve shape and the resulting image.

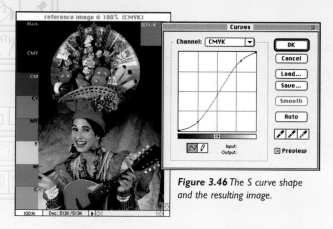

Figure 3.46 The S curve shape and the resulting image.

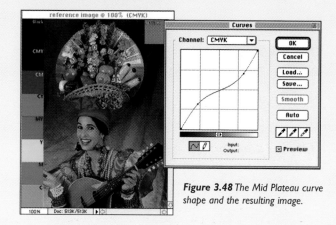

Figure 3.48 The Mid Plateau curve shape and the resulting image.

- Sharp Rise. Raising the highlights to an upper plateau results in a steeper curve in the 1/4 tones to mid tones. This can open up an image that's too dark, although it can also flatten out fine detail in the lightest highlights.
- Mid Plateau. Raising the shadows and lowering the highlights results in a chair-like shape with a flat plateau in the midtones. While a balanced image might suffer from this treatment, images that are primarily light or dark will benefit from the extra range this gives the lights and shadows.

- Inverted Straight Curve. Making a curve move from upper right to the lower left results in the inversion to a negative image. This does the same as the Invert command, although it does allow additional fine-tuning of the curve.
- Inverted S Curve. Modifying an inverted curve to show a backwards S results in a negative image with the heightened contrast characteristics of the aforementioned S curve.

(continued)

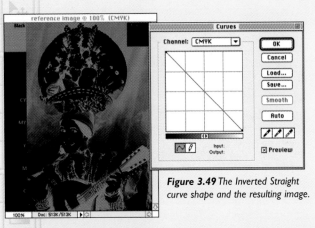

Figure 3.49 The Inverted Straight curve shape and the resulting image.

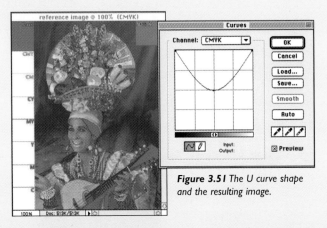

Figure 3.51 The U curve shape and the resulting image.

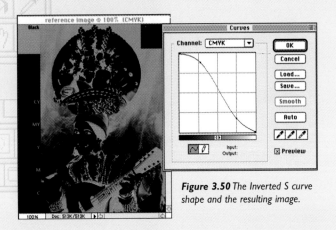

Figure 3.50 The Inverted S curve shape and the resulting image.

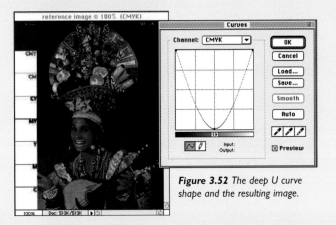

Figure 3.52 The deep U curve shape and the resulting image.

- The U Curve. Raising the highlights up to the top left shadow area results in an image where the midtones and highlights remain the same, while the shadows invert to highlight values.
- The Deep U Curve. In addition to raising the shadow point,

the deep U curve also lowers the midpoints to the shadows. At this point, the only tonal values that remain constant are the highlights, while the midtones go dark and the shadows go light.

Chapter 4

MASTERING LAYERS

The possibilities are endless, especially if you have a healthy chunk of RAM, a strong processor, and the desire to step through the looking glass.

At its most basic level, Photoshop displays a grid of pixels that your eye reinterprets as an image. For years this pixel grid worked so that if you moved one of the pixels, it was replaced by the background value. This replacement left the impression that the Photoshop image sat right on the surface, and the slightest scratch would dispel the illusion of depth, revealing the image to be a facade.

This impression led to vertical and horizontal thinking when it came to Photoshop designs. You could create things up, down, and across, but never into the third dimension. It never felt like there was any depth to the image. In some ways, Photoshop turned your computer into a $5000 Etch-A Sketch.

Photoshop version 3 was a bit more forgiving with the addition of the layers function. In retrospect, this first attempt at opening up the Y-axis was somewhat cumbersome, but Adobe has improved things a bit since then. At first layers made Photoshop work more like a Colorforms set, allowing you to composite in basic ways, but limiting how many layers you could comfortably work with. Like Colorforms, you could place objects on top of one another while keeping them separate, but the objects never seemed integrated.

The improvements since that first release have been a more intuitive memory management system, color correction layers, and easier access to layer controls. The end result is a design space you can finally conceptualize in three axes instead of just two (Figure 4.1). The artist needs to make the same mind-shift. You can integrate, separate, hide, and reveal with a casual deftness lacking until this latest release. Stop thinking in terms of the Etch-A Sketch and Colorforms, and step up to a 32-bit animated 3D video game. The possibilities are endless, especially if you have a healthy chunk of RAM, a strong processor, and the desire to step through the looking glass.

Figure 4.1 It is important to understand how layers allow you to work into the z-axis of the image.

The Layers Palette
and the Layers Menu

Adobe added a Layers menu to Photoshop 4. This menu has most of the same features as the Layers palette, with the addition of some Transform commands that used to be in the Image menu (Figure 4.2). Some like it, but to others it just seems excessive. When palettes were introduced to interfaces in the early 1990s, we were told that they would alleviate returning to a menu. To this end, Adobe presented an intuitive and easy-to-use palette system, which it then contradicted by creating a menu with the same features.

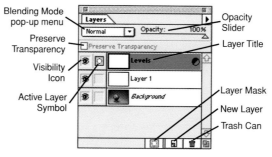

Figure 4.3 *The Layers palette.*

Figure 4.2 *The Layers menu commands.*

Because the Layers palette has the added benefit of visually organizing the actual layers, I will diagram the feature set there, calling out any individual differences in either the palette or the menu as they arise.

The Layers Palette

Activate the **Show Layers** command in the Windows menu, and you open up the Layers Palette. You are presented with a window that has a horizontal bar called *Background* (provided you have a file open), commands across the top, and two rows on the left side (Figure 4.3). As you add layers, they will stack up over the Background layer.

The far left column in the palette shows an eye symbol, which indicates whether or not a layer is visible. Click the eye and it disappears, along with the corresponding layer. Another click brings the layer and the eye symbol back into view. The next column to the right displays a paintbrush symbol to indicate the active layer that can be modified. The active layer is also a darker shade of gray. Click on any layer, either in the horizontal bar or in the paintbrush column, to activate it. Only one layer can be modified at a time.

The first layer in an image is always called the Background layer. Its opacity is always 100%, and it will not accept a layer mask. To get around this limit, you can either duplicate the background by selecting **Duplicate Layer** from the Layers Options palette, or double-click the background and save it as a layer. In the latter example, the image would have no background at all, which does not adversely effect the image.

At the very top of the palette is the Layer Blending mode pop-up menu, as well as an opacity slider. Moving the slider towards zero makes the active layer more transparent, revealing the layers underneath. The Layer Apply modes perform calculations between the active layer and those below it, and are discussed in more detail later.

The Preserve Transparency checkbox allows you to maintain a layer's transparency characteristics as it is modified. For example, if a layer is transparent except for an object, any edits would only affect the object, without modifying the transparent areas.

At the bottom of the palette are three other symbols: a trash can, folded corner pad, and a square with a circle inside it. The trash can deletes layers that are dragged onto it. The folded corner pad creates

a new layer when it is selected. The square with a circle inside activates a layer mask.

In the upper-right corner of the palette is a pop-up menu that allows you to create new layers and delete or duplicate existing ones (Figure 4.4). You also have the ability to merge layers together, either globally or just those visible. The Palette Options command modifies the way the palette displays information. The other command in this menu is Layer Options, which is a very powerful way to control how layers interact.

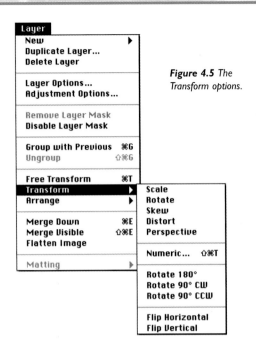

Figure 4.5 The Transform options.

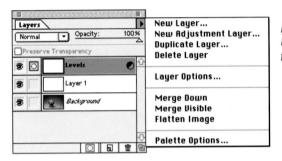

Figure 4.4 The Layers palette pop-up menu.

ment grid is getting twisted, pinched, or tweaked. The Numeric command delivers numeric precision to these commands, which is valuable when you need to apply the same degree of change to a number of layers (Figure 4.6).

The Layers Menu

The palette-based commands shoulder most of the initial layer creation, while the Layers menu tends to deliver controls for modifying existing layers. It delivers all of the functionality from the Layers palette pop-up menu, with a few additions. There are commands to create and enable layer masks, layer grouping commands, and a Matting command that enhances silhouetted layers.

The Transform Options

The Transform commands allow you to change the shape, size, and position of any given layer. As the Transform pop-up menu reveals, images can be rotated, scaled up or down, or distorted (Figure 4.5). You can also apply a perspective effect or skew the image. These first five effects are grouped in the menu because they all modify that pixel grid discussed earlier. The pixel values are unaltered, but the place-

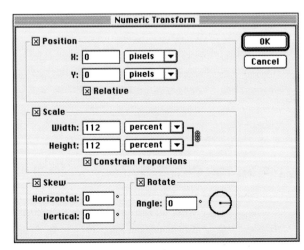

Figure 4.6 The Numeric dialog box from the Transform pop-up menu.

The last two Transform groups allow you to rotate a layer 90 degrees in either direction or to turn it upside down. The Flip commands reverse the image along the horizontal or vertical axis.

Given that users often perform a sequence of Transform moves at one time, such as rotating and scaling an image, Adobe included a Free Transform command in the Photoshop 4 release. This command lets you rotate and scale the image as part of a single command. Position the mouse on the side handles to scale the layer from just that side. The corner points allow scaling of two sides, with the **Shift** key constraining proportions. To rotate the object, move the cursor off the handle points until it turns into the rotate icon. Once you have the image where you want it, double-click the center of the image or click on the **Move** tool, and click **OK** to apply the changes.

Basic Layer Tasks

Knowing where the layer commands are, we can move on to the more important task of properly using the controls at our disposal. You should know basics such as how to create various layer types and how to delete, duplicate, and move layers about your image. In addition, you should be familiar with how to drag layers to change their order in the layer stack. See your Photoshop manual for this information. Dispensing with the basic layer functions, we can focus on how to work with layers in developing intuitive workflow.

Working with layers can be broken into three broad categories: creating and accessing source material, modifying and enhancing the material on a single layer, and integrating multiple layers back together. Some of these steps are more important than others, depending on the type of image you're creating. The various image types are discussed in the next section, along with comments on how this manipulation approach would vary.

Creating and Enhancing Source Material

At first glance, it may appear that this subject is out of place in a section on working with layers. This section refers to Photoshop's ability to generate multiple copies of an image, each in a separate layer.

These layers can be modified in various ways and put back together to form a single image. In this way, these layer copies serve as individual source material components. This is slightly different from what we looked at in Chapter 1, where we copied the image to a layer as a safety net.

For example, you may want to enhance the color of the grass in the background of an image. Layers allow you to copy the grass or the entire image to a new layer, enhance the green in just that layer, and integrate it with the foreground. This keeps the edited version separate from the original image and allows further modification if necessary. There are many ways to create multiple versions, some of which are listed next.

SELECTING PASTE

The most obvious way to generate new source material in a new layer is to copy and paste. When the Paste command places an object in the image, a new layer appears in the Layers palette, numbered sequentially. This eliminates what was once a problem with Photoshop, in that the pasted object would accidentally get stuck in the wrong place by being deselected. If you're pasting a lot, be sure to flatten or merge your layers to keep the file at a manageable size and to keep the number of layers to a minimum.

DUPLICATING LAYERS

When creating color or tonal effects in a naturalistic image, duplicating the image several times can create the source material needed to make the various changes. If you want an image with a soft background and sharp foreground, create two duplicates of your image, then sharpen one image layer and blur the other. With the original as the bridge between them, you now have foreground, middle ground, and background sources from which you can make a composite (Figure 4.7). We'll talk about compositing later, but the first step is to duplicate the layer.

To duplicate a layer, select **Duplicate Layer** from the Layers palette pop-up menu or the Layers menu. The dialog box that appears asks for the new layer name, and the destination for the layer (Figure 4.8). To select an alternative destination file, it must be open at the time the layer is duplicated.

Figure 4.7 *With the same image on multiple layers, one version can be blurred and the other sharpened. The combined result is a focus effect that remains modifiable at all times.*

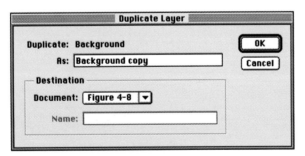

Figure 4.8 *The Duplicate Layer dialog box.*

MULTIPLE SCANS AND PHOTOGRAPHS

An alternative to creating multiple layers of the same image, multiple scans of the same image can be created to be similarly composited. If the original photo or chrome is of high quality, consider making two or three scans that emphasize certain tonal areas. Emphasizing the shadows in one file and the highlights in another would create separate files of the same image with different tonal emphasis. As long as they are scanned at the same size and resolution, i.e., the same pixel dimension, you can bring each file in as a layer and integrate the best parts of each image.

Taking this philosophy one step further is the idea of using multiple photographs. Imagine taking sequential photos where the objects do not move, but the lighting changes. This could allow for some very interesting effects, either toward abstraction or image enhancement.

The result of all of these techniques is the isolation of the areas you wish to enhance. It is similar to a selection, except that the original source material is left untouched. All that's left is to modify the various layers and integrate them. Multiple scans or photographs may not need further modification, leaving nothing to do except the integration.

Ways to Enhance the Versions

What you do to an image once it's in a layer depends on your overall goal of the design. To create a conventional montage from different images, bring the images together so that they feel a part of the same design, add a texture or filter treatment to all of the layers, or tweak the color so that all of the elements appear to be lit from the same light source. These steps would homogenize the image, making it more cohesive. Alternatively, you may duplicate the same image into multiple layers in order to modify specific areas of the image. In this instance, your goal would be to enhance specific areas and differentiate them from the source image.

Whether differentiating or homogenizing, you need to be aware of all your options as you set about modifying the layers you've created. All options entail some combination of modifying the color, sharpness, or texture of the layer.

RECIPE: TAPE SILHOUETTE

Some of the best composites you'll ever see are those that you don't even recognize. The ability to use multiple images as sources of information can really aid your designs.

As an example, during an ad photo shoot, a photographer moving lights around the setup happened to backlight the subject in a very interesting way. The image was dramatic, but there was no detail on the subject, a tape cartridge (Figure 4.9). When the photographer boasted that he could light it for detail at the expense of several hours of the shoot, I opted for the digital approach.

Without disturbing the initial setup, the scene was relit from the front and the image was reshot (Figure 4.10). With the two images positioned the same way, but lit completely differently, it was time to let Photoshop do the rest:

Figure 4.9 The initial tape shot with dramatic lighting.

Figure 4.10 The same setup, fully lit from the front.

1. The front-lit tape image is opened and zoomed to 100%.
2. The Path tool is selected from the toolbox, and a path is drawn around the cassette itself.
3. Rather than making one complex path around everything in the image, separate paths were drawn around the cascading tape. One path is drawn around the upper loop, and another is drawn going down towards the tabletop. These three sub-

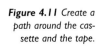

RECIPE: CONTINUED

paths all exist as part of the Path named Cassette and are activated simultaneously as needed (Figure 4.11).

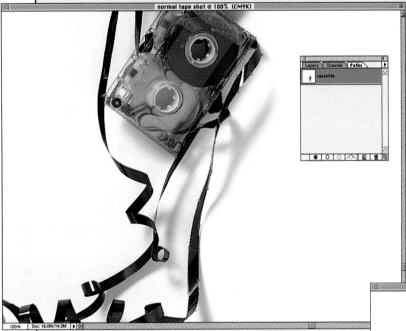

Figure 4.11 Create a path around the cassette and the tape.

7. To remove the white patch in the tape loop, a Layer Mask is created. This is a case where erasing only makes things worse, because of the way the Luminosity Apply Mode interacts with the layer below. With the upper layer selected, click on the Layer Mask icon at the bottom of the screen. This creates a transparent (white) layer mask where the entire contents of the layer are visible.

8. Because black masks the contents of the active layer, black is set to the background color and the eraser is selected. The Airbrush eraser option is selected, and the white area is masked (Figure 4.14). Any paintbrush tool with black as the foreground color would have produced this same effect.

The final effect is an image with a wide tonal range and fine detail throughout. It would have taken hours to set the lighting the same way, if even possible. Rather than pay a photographer to juggle light stands, just think ahead and have enough confidence in your skills to take multiple shots (Figure 4.15).

4. The Cassette path is converted to a selection with the **Make Selection** command from the Paths palette submenu, and the selection is copied (Figure 4.12).

5. The dramatically lit tape image is opened, and the copied selection is pasted. This selection automatically comes in as a separate layer.

6. The Luminosity Apply Mode is then selected, which lets some of the yellow color show through the back of the tape, further uniting the two layers. The opacity slider is also reduced down to 69% (Figure 4.13).

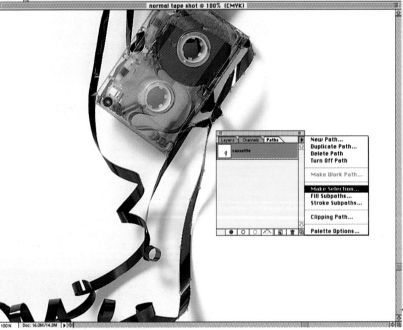

Figure 4.12 Convert the path to a selection.

Figure 4.13 The selection comes in as a separate layer.

Figure 4.15 The final composite result.

Figure 4.14 Using a Layer Mask
to eliminate the white fringe.

CURVES AND COLOR TWEAKS

You can modify the color in a layer with any of the color tools we looked at in Chapter 3. Reasons to tweak a layer's color include the following:

- Create a similar light source. In collaging a person in a beach scene at sunset, the person will probably look cut out and artificial. The lighting at sunset is very distinct and unless the image of the person was taken at the same time or place, it will probably not look right. Sunset light has a reddish yellow color, while interior light is more of a pale yellow. Fluorescent lighting appears greenish, and midday light is neutral to slightly bluish. Be aware of this and be sure to modify the images you're integrating so they share the same light source (Figure 4.16).

Figure 4.16 Layers that appear to share the same light source look more cohesive and believable.

- Enhancing certain colors. Once you have an identical image duplicated to several layers, you may want to use one of the layers to enhance the color of a specific object or area. Perhaps it's to make the grass a little greener, or to bring out the reds in apples on the table. It's simple to globally modify the entire layer with Curves or Levels, then erase or tone down everything except the object you're enhancing. This can be a simple alternative to selecting the area and modifying it all on the same layer, and allows you to take more risks without modifying the original data.

- Dramatic color changes. Maybe you want every object in the image to be blue, but the only crayon image you have is red. This is more than a simple cast change. Follow the same basic approach as the example on enhancing certain colors, but you would use the Hue/Saturation command in the **Image: Adjust** submenu. Once in this dialog, check the **Colorize** box in the lower-right corner and move the Hue slider at the top to access the desired color.
- Remove all the color. A single colored object looks dramatic against a grayscale background (Figure 4.17). To do this, duplicate the image into two layers and erase all of one layer except for the object to be emphasized. Convert the other layer to grayscale by selecting **Desaturate**. To remove only some of the color from the grayscale layer, open the **Hue/Saturation** command in the **Image: Adjust** menu, and slide the Saturation slider to the left.

Figure 4.17 Spot color in a grayscale image acts as a very effective focal point.

RECIPE: MAKING AN OBLECT GLOW

Taking an object that is lit from the outside and making it look like it is lit from within is no easy task. It is a matter of changing the light source from external to internal, without sacrificing color or detail. The method described here should work for most objects and situations, although certain tweaks may be necessary as the subject matter varies.

Main points to remember are that the object should be in a darker environment and the saturation should be higher than normal. Then it's really a matter of combining the various details until the proper balance is achieved.

1. Begin by selecting the entire image and copying it to a new layer. To do this, select **Duplicate Layer** from the Layers Palette Options menu (Figure 4.18).
2. Select the object as carefully as possible, and choose **Select: Save Selection** to save the selection to a new channel.

3. In the Layers palette, turn off the visibility in the top layer and click on the bottom to activate it.
4. Choose **Select All** from the Select menu, and select **Layer: Transform: Numeric** and set the scale values at 125%. Make sure that the Constrain Proportions box is checked and click **OK**, then choose **Select: None** to defloat the selection (Figure 4.19).
5. With the entire bottom layer selected, choose **Filter: Blur: Radial Blur**. In this case, the slider was set to 47%, the method at Zoom; and the quality level at Best (Figure 4.20). Click **OK** to apply the effect.

Figure 4.19 Scale the image to 125% using the Numeric Transform option.

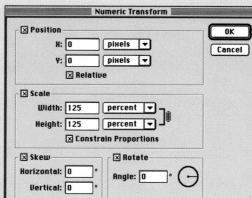

Figure 4.18 Duplicate the entire image to a new layer.

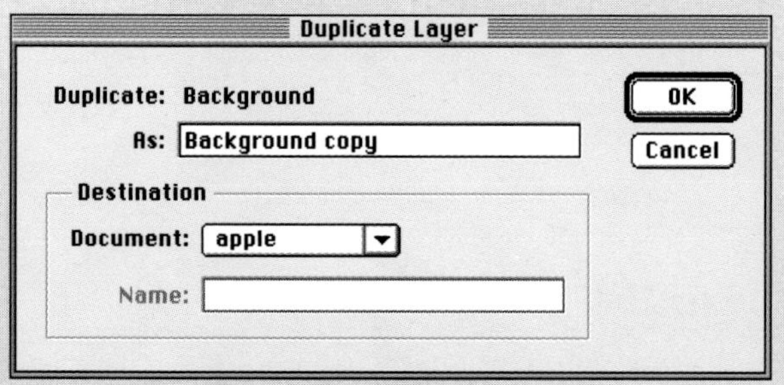

Figure 4.20 Apply a Radial Blur to the Background Layer

RECIPE: ─ **CONTINUED**

6. Select **Image: Adjust: Invert** to shift the image to a dark, radiant background.

7. In the Layers palette, click on the top layer and choose **Select: Load Selection**, and specify #4 in the Channel pop-up menu. Check the **Invert** box and the **New Selection** radio button. Click **OK** to load the selection, and press the **Delete** key to delete the background (Figure 4.21).

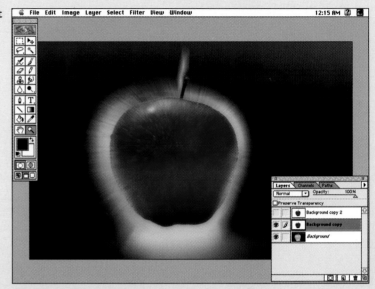

Figure 4.22 Apply a radial blur to Layer 2.

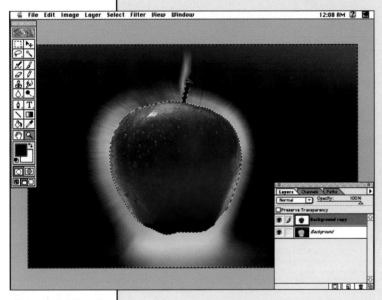

Figure 4.21 Delete the background in Layer 2.

8. Duplicate the second layer by selecting **Duplicate Layer** from the Layers options menu, turn off the visibility in the top layer, and click on the middle layer to activate it.

9. Choose **Select: Feather** to feather the selection, specifying a feather radius of 25 pixels. Click **OK** to apply the feather.

10. Choose **Select: Invert** to invert the selection to just the apple, then select **Filter: Blur: Radial Blur** and move the slider to 25%. With **Zoom** and **Best** quality selected, click **OK** (Figure 4.22).

11. With the middle layer still active, select **Image: Adjust: Invert**. Then select **Image: Adjust: Hue/Saturation** and check the col-

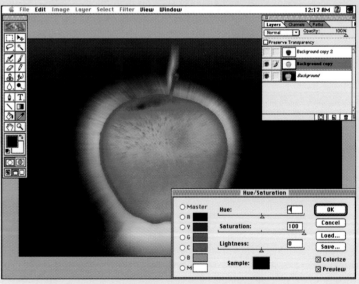

Figure 4.23 Colorize Layer 2 through the Hue/Saturation dialog box.

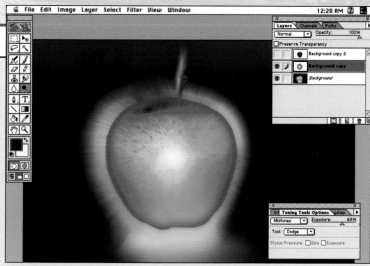

Figure **4.24** *Select the **Dodge** tool and lighten the center of the apple.*

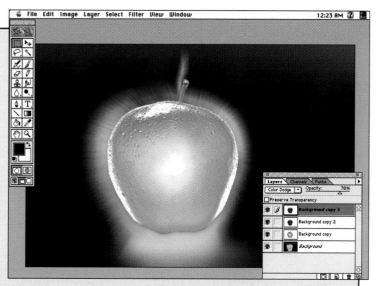

Figure **4.25** *Set the top Layer Apply mode to **Color Dodge** at 78% opacity.*

orize box, moving the Hue slider to +4 (Figure 4.23). Click **OK** to apply the effect.

12. Double-click the Toning tool to activate the Dodge/Burn options menu. Set the tone area to **Midtones**, the tool setting at **Dodge**, and the **Exposure** slider to 69%. Select a large brush and lighten the center of the middle layer to a brighter white (Figure 4.24).

13. Click on the top layer and duplicate it. At this point you should have four layers, the bottom two with altered colors, the top two

with natural colors. Click on the third layer from the bottom to activate it and select **Screen** from the Apply Mode pop-up menu.

14. Click on the top layer to activate it, select **Color Dodge** from the Apply Mode pop-up menu, and move the Opacity slider to 78% (Figure 4.25).

15. Click on the bottom layer to activate it, choose **Select: None**, and select **Image: Adjust: Color Balance**. Click on the **Shadows** radio button and move the top slider to +38 red/cyan, the middle slider to -17 magenta/green, and the bottom slider to -16 yellow/blue.

16. Click on the **Midtones** radio button and move the top slider to +21 red/cyan, the middle slider to -16 magenta/green, and the bottom slider to 0 yellow/blue. Click the **highlights** radio button and set the top slider to +1 red/cyan, the middle slider to -33 magenta/green, and the bottom slider to -3 yellow/blue (Figure 4.26).

Figure **4.27** *The final image.*

The final image still retains much of the detail and sharpness as the original, while giving off quite a convincing glow. The red background infers the original color of the object and the overall contrast is about right. Depending on the context and how much detail you're after, you may choose to blur back the glowing rays from the bottom layer, creating a softer light (Figure 4.27).

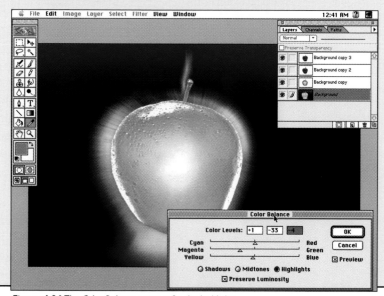

Figure **4.26** *The Color Balance settings for the highlights.*

SHARPEN AND BLUR

Sharpening and blurring modify the relative values of adjacent pixels, enhancing or obscuring the detail in the image. The tools to sharpen and blur an image are found primarily in the filters menu, in the Sharpen and Blur submenus. In addition to these areas, you can also sharpen and blur an image with the KPT 3.0 Edge fx, Smudge fx, and Texture Explorer. KPT Convolver gives tremendous control over the sharpness and texture of an image, as do the Alien Skin filters and many other third-party offerings.

Use the sharpening and blurring effects to bring out details in your image as you need to. Other ideas and methods for specialized sharpening and blurring effects include:

- Sharpen an image on a blurred background. Isolating and sharpening an image on one layer while blurring the rest of the image on another layer can be as effective as the color/grayscale effect mentioned previously. This technique is a bit more subtle and naturalistic, and if handled right it can emulate the depth of field effects of a view camera (Figures 4.28 A and B).

- Emulate atmospheric perspective. *Atmospheric perspective* refers to the way a landscape appears softer and lighter as it recedes. The closer an object, the more it is in sharp focus with solid contrast. You can emulate this effect by duplicating the same image into multiple layers, blurring one, and sharpening the other. The integration is key in this effect, as we will discuss in the next section.

Figures 4.28 A and B *Layers facilitate the creation of subtle or powerful depths of field effects.*

RECIPE: ZOOM LENS BLUR

This recipe simulates the zoom lens exposure effects you see in all the photography magazines, in which a background is blurred to a center point. In the traditional photography method, a camera with a zoom lens is mounted on a tripod and pointed at the subject. The shutter is then locked open for a long exposure, as the lens is zoomed in on the subject. Digital methods allow us to achieve this same effect with any image, in a much simpler way.

Figure 4.30
The Take Snapshot command.

1. An image with this much clutter benefits from this effect by creating a focal point and framing the subject matter (Figure 4.29). After opening the image, save a copy as a Snapshot by selecting **Edit: Take Snapshot** (Figure 4.30).

2. Select **Filter: Blur: Radial Blur**. In the dialog box, select **Zoom** as a blur method and **Good** in the quality settings. An important

Figure 4.29 The original image.

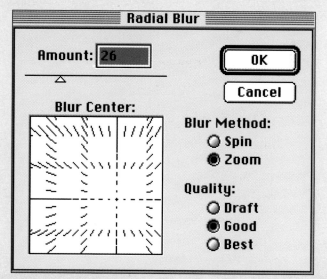

Figure 4.31 The Radial Blur dialog box.

step is to click and drag the zoom center to correspond with where the zoom should go to in your image. In this example, the zoom center was moved to fall on the one soldier that would be the focal point (Figure 4.31). As a result, the entire image is blurred into the focal point (Figure 4.32).

3. Double-click on the **Rubber Stamp** tool to open the Rubber Stamp Options palette. Set the Options to **From Snapshot,** the Opacity at 100%, and the Apply Mode to **normal.** Double click on the **Magnifying Glass** to magnify the image to 100%, and paint back the sharpened version of the soldier (Figures 4.33 and 4.34).

Figure 4.33 Zoom to 100% and paint back the center subject from the Snapshot mode.

4. To add additional focus on the soldier, select **Image: Adjust: Curves** and increase the highlights and lower the shadows in a standard "S" curve. (Figure 4.35) Figure 4.36 shows the final image.

Figure 4.32 The results of the radial blur.

Figure 4.34 The results of step 3.

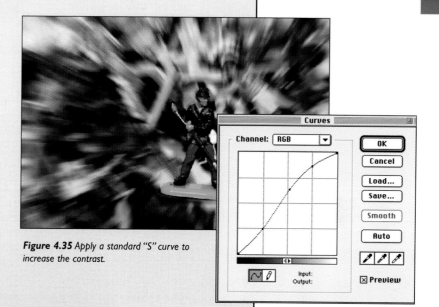

Figure 4.35 Apply a standard "S" curve to increase the contrast.

Figure 4.36 The final image.

USE APPLY MODE LAYERS

The New Layer command, also in the Layers palette and menu, lets you generate a layer that acts as an Apply mode for whatever is below it, even if it's just one layer. This is significant in that the Apply modes always require two superimposed pixel values, such as two layers, or pixels from a paste and original file. Before this option was added, there was no way to apply a Difference effect to one layer since there was only one pixel value.

To create an Apply mode layer, be sure to select any mode other then Normal from the Modes pop-up menu. Remember that in the case of a new layer, it will come in with no associated source material. If that's the case, the alternate pixel value for the effect comes by checking the bottom **Fill with** box in the dialog, filling the layer with a neutral color (Figure 4.37). The exact checkbox wording and fill color depend on the mode selected, but the color generated is designed to apply the effect to the underlying layers.

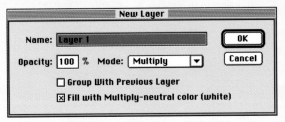

Figure 4.37 *Selecting any mode but Normal activates the* **Fill with** *option, allowing the layer and mode selection to be applied.*

USE ADJUSTMENT LAYERS

Purists will protest the inclusion of Adjustment Layer effects in this section on modifying individual layers. They will argue that Adjustment Layers are independent of the actual layers they modify and act like filters, altering how the underlying layers are displayed.

This is true. The Adjustment Layers are included here because they deliver the same results, and fit into the same process as the other effects in this section. It should be known, however, that they are a hybrid, allowing the modification of a single layer or group of layers with any of the color controls.

Adjustment Layers alter all of the layers beneath them, applying the effects as desired. Other than the obvious reasons for using Adjustment Layers, there are some specific approaches that can work to your advantage. Most of these rely on the fact that Adjustment Layer effects are cumulative, building on those beneath them. Some alternate approaches include:

- Stagger identical Adjustment Layers. You can intersperse identical Adjustment Layers throughout the layer stack, intensifying the effect as objects recede into the layer stack. This allows you to specify objects or areas that are more intensely colored than others, depending on how many adjustment layers are above them.
- Invert images. An Adjustment Layer can create a negative image of what's below it in several ways. You can select **Invert** from the pop-up menu, which automatically delivers the results desired. This can be limiting however, and you might prefer to select the Curves option, manually reversing the curve to a negative shape (Figure 4.38). In this way, you can heighten the contrast in certain areas and further control how the inversion is applied.

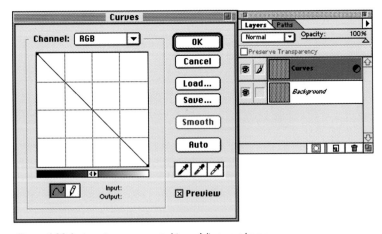

Figure 4.38 *An inversion curve created in an Adjustment Layer.*

RECIPE: STAINED GLASS ANGEL

This image was developed by experimenting with the cumulative effects of the Adjustment Layers. Because the effects are compounded as they stack up, the results can be surprising and beautiful.

1. The initial image is a stock photo of an angel. The tonal range is not that deep, and the overall image is not very striking (Figure 4.39).

Figure 4.39 The original stock photo of the angel.

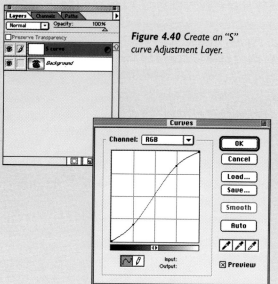

Figure 4.40 Create an "S" curve Adjustment Layer.

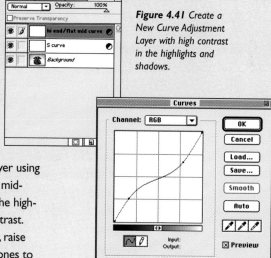

Figure 4.41 Create a New Curve Adjustment Layer with high contrast in the highlights and shadows.

2. Create a Curves Adjustment layer of a standard "S" curve, which deepens the shadows and brightens the highlights, while increasing the tonal contrast in the midtones. To do this, select **New Adjustment Layer** from the Layers Options palette. Make sure **Curves** is showing in the Type pop-up menu and click **OK**. When the Curves window appears, create an "S" curve to the degree necessary. Follow this procedure for the creation of all Adjustment Layers in this recipe (Figure 4.40).

3. Create a New Curves Adjustment Layer using a curve with flattened contrast in the midtones. This creates steeper slopes in the highlights and shadows, increasing the contrast. When the Curves dialog box appears, raise the quartertones and lower the 3/4 tones to create this inverted "S" curve effect (Figure 4.41).

RECIPE: CONTINUED

4. Create an inverted "S" Curve Adjustment Layer. To do this, drag the lower left beginning curve point to the upper-left corner. At this point, there is a straight line across the top. Click on the upper-right point of the curve and drag it to the lower right. This will create a negative of the image, which can be further modified by raising the quartertones and lowering the 3/4 tones, creating the same "S" shape as before, only going in the other direction (Figure 4.42).

Figure 4.42 Create an inverted "S" curve Adjustment Layer.

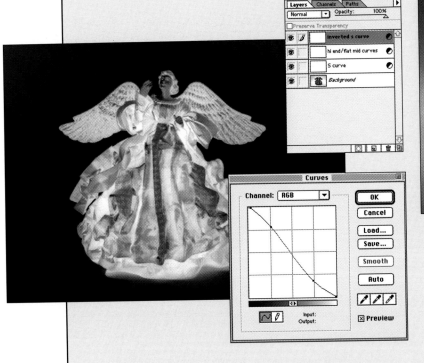

5. Create an inverted Curve Adjustment Layer of the curve created in step three. Select **New Adjustment Layer** from the Layer submenu, Invert the curve as in the previous step, and flatten the midtones while stretching the highlights and shadow.

6. Create another Curves Adjustment Layer, this time for experimental purposes. The settings below yielded this dramatic effect, which we'll call *oil slick* (Figure 4.43).

Figure 4.43 The curve shown yielded this effect, reminiscent of an oil slick.

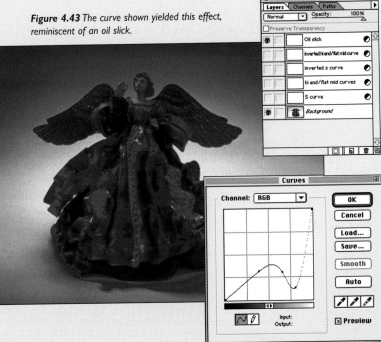

7. The layers were shuffled to arrive at the final combination of Adjustment Layers. All of the curves were used except for the inverted flat midcurve created in step 5 (Figure 4.44).

8. To finish the effect, paint in an Adjustment Layer mask to intensify the hands, wings, and head of the angel (Figure 4.45). To do this, select an airbrush with black as the active foreground color. Painting black over the top oil slick Adjustment Layer masks out its effects, revealing the image as it appears in the layers below (Figure 4.46)

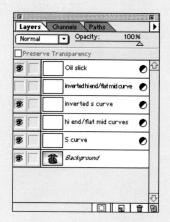

Figure 4.44 The
Layers palette shows
the final order and
usage for the
Adjustment Layers
used in this effect.

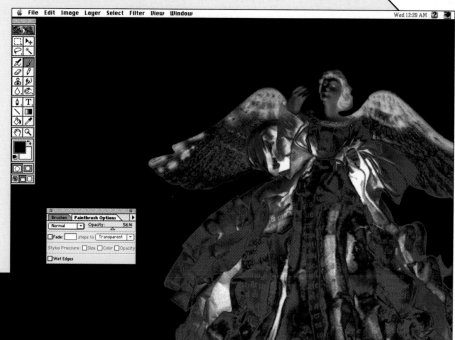

Figure 4.45 Painting
a Layer Mask for the
oil slick Adjustment
Layer.

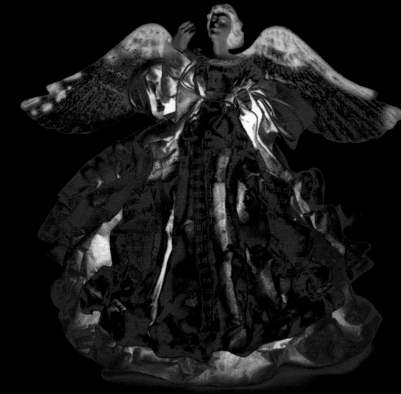

Figure 4.46
The final image.

• Create low contrast images. Creating a low-contrast Adjustment Layer effect can be effective for a number of reasons. It has already been mentioned that you can emphasize an object by de-emphasizing everything else (Figure 4.47). In addition, creating a low-contrast version of the image can generate more dramatic Apply Mode effects between layers.

Figure 4.47 *With the bottom layer reduced to very low-contrast, the full-contrast face area was painted in from a second layer with the help of a layer mask.*

Ways to Integrate Versions

There is little advantage to working magic on individual layers if they don't all flow back together as a cohesive unit. Managing the transitions between the visible areas in the image determines how convincing, crafted, or effective the final piece is. The goal is to have all of the image components work together seamlessly without calling attention to how something was accomplished. It's similar to a special effect in a movie, where if it is done correctly you just believe it, without stepping back to figure out how it was done.

BASIC BLENDING OPTIONS

In Chapter 2 we looked at how the edge determined how an object should be selected. The same analysis applies in combining layers. You need to ask yourself if you want a hard edge, soft edge, or lost edge between the layer objects. The answer will usually give you a hint as to the approach you should take in combining the layers.

One of the easiest ways to integrate two or more layers is to erase the portion of the uppermost layer, letting the lower ones show through. This can be difficult if the areas to be Erased have crisp, well-defined edges, as tracing an object's edge with the eraser tool is not so easy. The Block eraser, for example, does not match up well here.

If the object has a softer edge, then the Airbrush tool can be quite effective. When going in with the Airbrush Eraser, try to use the largest brush possible, actually dabbing the eraser into an area. In working this way, you can hide the traces of the hand and brush. If possible, I like to use a 500+ pixel brush to really work a large area smoothly.

Remember that there is an opacity slider in the Eraser Options palette that controls how much of an image is erased. Use this to create as smooth a transition as possible.

If the Eraser tool is great for soft edge transitions, then the Paths tool is perfect for the hard-edged effects. When converting a path to a selection try and specify as much of a feather as the image will bear. The great thing with paths is that the lines and Bezier curves smoothly articulate an object's edge and actually let you get away with more of a feathered edge than normally possible.

Given that a path is repeatable and savable, there may actually be times where you can use the same path on two different layers to facilitate the same transition. For example, you could create a path around an object, feather a selection, and delete the background. Then select the layer below the object, reactivate the path, and make the same feathered selection, this time inverting it. You now can soften or delete the area just below the first object's edges, making the combination more convincing.

BLENDING OPTIONS IN THE LAYERS PALETTE

The basic blending options covered ways to combine layers using Photoshop's standard tool set. In addition to these options, Adobe has built various blending options right into the Layers palette. These options are not quite as intuitive as the basic set, but they do offer some unique possibilities that the basic approaches just can't match.

The Opacity slider at the top of the Layers palette also appears in the Layer Option dialog box. Adding transparency is a very basic way of integrating multiple layers together, especially for more abstract and montage effects.

Select **Layer Options** from the Layers palette pop-up menu to modify opacity or layer Apply modes. There is also a Threshold control that dictates how the current layer combines with those below (Figure 4.48). The Opacity and Apply modes are available at all times at the top of the Layers palette, but the Threshold options are quite unique. (See Chapter 5 for a full explanation of how the Apply modes work).

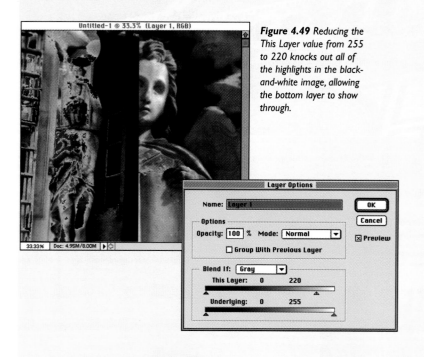

Figure 4.49 Reducing the This Layer value from 255 to 220 knocks out all of the highlights in the black-and-white image, allowing the bottom layer to show through.

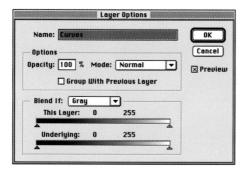

Figure 4.48 The Layer Options dialog box.

The top slider represents the tonal range of the current layer, while the slider below it represents the rest of the image. By adjusting the top slider, you can knock out the pixel values in the top layer, letting the lower image layers come through. Moving the white slider from 255 to 220 means that all of the pixels over 220 in the current layer will disappear, and the layer(s) below 220 will become visible (Figure 4.49). You are reducing the tonal range of the current layer, and the clipped pixels are being made transparent.

The lower slider works in the opposite way. The pixels below push their way into the active layer, depending on the values selected. For example, moving the lower slider from 255 to 220 will make all of the light pixels from 221 to 255 sit up on top of the current layer, replacing whatever was above them.

For even more control, Photoshop allows you to make these adjustments on the individual RGB/CMYK color channels. This would allow you to knock out all of the red pixel values over 200, for example, or let the cyan pixels in the shadow areas come forward. These Layer Options often produce a solarized effect, without much subtlety or finesse. It can be hard to control how the effect is applied, as it tends to abstract the entire layer, rather than just modifying the spots you might like. On the other hand, these can be powerful tools for the right kind of image, especially for objects with sharper edges or where the lights and darks in the image are clearly delineated.

CHANNEL BLENDS

For some montage effects, you may want a fade between layers that does not follow a specific object or area. A fade that originates in a channel selection can easily handle this requirement. This is done by selecting **New Channel** from the Channels palette, and creating a blend that goes from black to white (Figure 4.50). In a new channel, black serves to mask the contents of the image, while white areas reveals what's there.

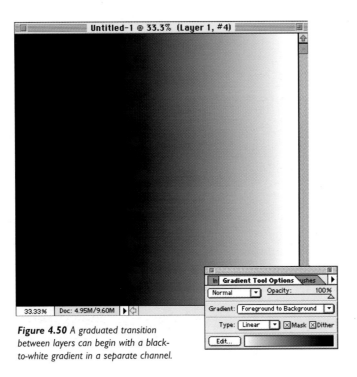

Figure 4.50 *A graduated transition between layers can begin with a black-to-white gradient in a separate channel.*

To activate the selection and create the transition, activate the full-image composite channel, and select **Load Selection** from the Select menu, choosing the channel with the gradient (Figure 4.51).

Photoshop then selects all of the white areas in the channel to load as a selection, reducing the selection intensity as the white pixels fade to gray. At this point, you can use your favorite tool to delete or alter the selected areas.

Figure 4.51 *With the gradient channel loaded as a selection, the top layer can be faded using any number of Photoshop's Image/Adjust tools.*

The advantage to using channels, as opposed to converting a path to a selection is that the area selected can be modified with a paintbrush and eraser in a very specific way. In this sense, it is similar to the Quick Mask feature, except that the Quick Mask must at some point be converted to a selection. In contrast, a channel selection is always editable with the paint tools, it is always fluid. Keep in mind that a channel increases file size dramatically, so use channel selections with some discretion.

LAYER MASKS

Layer Masks are an automated way to use the channel selection method just described. With a basic understanding of how channel selections are made, Layer Masks should be clearer and easier to use.

When it comes to integrating multiple layers with each other, nothing comes close to the power of Layer Masks. Layer Masks deliver an extra level of control and accuracy that the channel selections withheld. The reason is that rather than having to jump to the Channels palette, paint a Channel Mask, activate it through the Selections menu, and hope the mask is where you want it. Layer Masks allow you to just push a button.

With one action, you have a choice of four options in starting your mask:

- Hiding the entire layer with a mask.
- Revealing the entire layer, with nothing masked.
- Hiding all of a layer except for an existing selection.
- Revealing an entire layer except for an existing selection.

The first two options are really two sides of the same coin, either paint the desired image back into the layer or erase the unwanted areas from the revealed image. At times it can be easier to start with a selection, especially if there is a path already drawn, or an easily selectable area. In the case of a selection, the same options of revealing or hiding the selected area exist, as mentioned in the bulleted list.

Creating and Understanding Layer Masks

To create a Layer Mask, you first need to make sure that the target layer for the mask is highlighted. If you want to base the mask on a selection, you should now select the desired area. At this point, you can either create a mask through the Add Layer Mask command in the Layers menu, or click on the Mask icon at the bottom of the Layers palette. The Add Layer Mask command in the Layers menu offers a submenu to choose from the four options just mentioned, while the Mask icon automatically creates a mask that reveals the

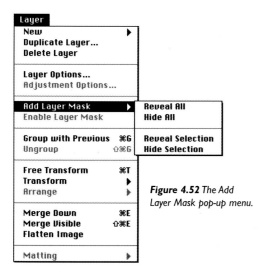

Figure 4.52 *The Add Layer Mask pop-up menu.*

entire layer (Figure 4.52). **Option**-click (Mac) or **Alt**-click (Windows) the Mask icon to create a mask that conceals the entire layer. If a selection is active, **Option**-clicking the Mask icon creates a mask that hides the selection.

In a Layer Mask, it is important to remember that black conceals the layer and white reveals it. Keep this in mind as you notice the mask thumbnail that appears next to the layer image thumbnail in the Layers palette. Its black-and-white areas correspond to the visible areas in the layer. If you click on the mask thumbnail, you may alter the mask, but not the image. Clicking back on the image thumbnail restores full editing control over the layer itself. The active mask or image thumbnails are highlighted with a black frame to help you keep track of what mode you're in.

Painting into a Layer Mask If a mask can be edited with white and black, it stands to reason that Photoshop's painting tools can be very valuable in fine-tuning a mask. With the mask thumbnail selected, you can use any of Photoshop's tools that create or alter black-and-white pixels. In addition to the Paintbrush and Airbrush, which are obvious choices, the Smudge, Sharpen, and Toning tools can also be effective.

To use Photoshop's paint tools, you would select the mask thumbnail, make sure that white or black is active in the color swatches, and paint into the image. When you create a Layer Mask, Photoshop automatically changes the color options to grayscale, reflecting the Channel Mask that is active at the time. It can be strange to paint into an image with black selected, only to see the image disappear under your brush. Having it appear from nowhere with white selected is also kind of disorienting (Figure 4.53).

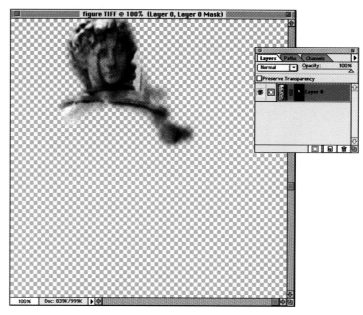

Figure 4.53 *With white selected, Layer Masks allow you to paint an image directly into the composition.*

As you work, you can temporarily turn a Layer Mask on or off by **Shift**-clicking the mask thumbnail, or selecting Mask Enabled from the Layers menu. If you would rather edit the mask without looking at the image in the layer, you can **Option**-click (Mac) or **Alt**-Click (Windows) the layer mask thumbnail to view just the grayscale mask. Like the Quick Mask feature, you can see the entire layer with a colored film over the remaining image layer by selecting **Option-** or **Alt**-shift, and clicking on the mask thumbnail (Figure 4.54). The default film color is red, but you can change this by double-clicking the Quick Mask icon and clicking the color swatch, and choosing another color.

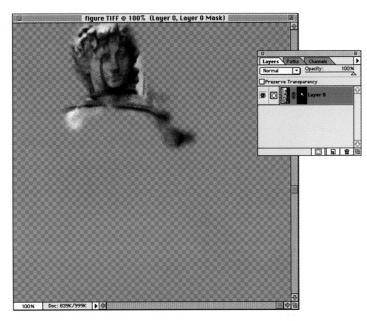

Figure 4.54 Click the layer mask thumbnail while holding down the **Option** (Mac) or **Alt** (Windows keys to see the Layer Mask superimposed over the image).

Given that Layer Masks are channel selections with an express line to the Layers palette, your files can get pretty large if you use too many of them. To keep files small and nimble, Photoshop will allow

you to apply or discard the mask at any time. To remove the mask, highlight the mask thumbnail and either click on the trash icon at the bottom of the Layers palette or select **Remove Layer Mask** from the Layers menu. The ensuing dialog prompts you to apply the mask to the layer or discard the mask, leaving the layer untouched (Figure 4.55).

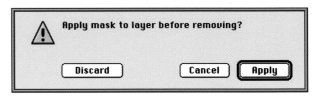

Figure 4.55 Apply Layer Masks as often as possible to keep file size low.

Layer Clipping Groups Imagine taking a Layer Mask and applying it to a series of layers. Photoshop delivers that capability with something called *Clipping Groups*. Clipping Groups behave similarly to a Layer Mask in that they conceal and reveal different areas of the image. The difference between Clipping Groups and Layer Masks is that Clipping Groups mask out all of the adjoining layers above the initial layer in the group.

While Layer Masks create grayscale channels that determine what's visible, Clipping Groups are determined by the opaque and transparent areas of the lowermost layer in the group. The area hidden in the bottom layer is hidden in all of the adjoining upper layers. This means that visible areas on an otherwise transparent lower layer would restrict all upper-layer effects to being inside the area.

It's similar to checking the Preserve Transparency box when you modify a layer, only the modifications are kept on separate layers. Remember that the Opacity sliders and Apply modes between layers still work within Clipping Groups, allowing you to maintain full control as you work.

To create a Clipping Group you need to establish a base layer and then group adjoining upper layers to the base. Establish the base layer for a Clipping Group in the Layers palette by placing the cursor on

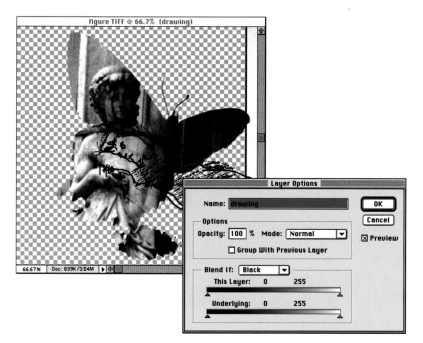

Figure 4.56 *Add a layer to an existing Clipping Group by double-clicking the layer and checking the **Group With Previous** box.*

Conclusion

the line dividing the base layer from the ones above it, and **Option**- (Mac) or **Alt**- (Windows) clicking. A dotted line appears above the base layer, and the image thumbnail in the layer above it is indented to the right. To group adjoining layers to the base layer, double-click the layer in the palette and check Group With Previous in the dialog box (Figure 4.56).

Since their inception, Layers have become an indispensable Photoshop tool. Whether you are enhancing a normative image, creating a montage, or going completely abstract, layers can make your work a lot easier. In combination with optimization, selection skills and color mastery, layers provide the final component in an intuitive workflow strategy.

part

2 PIXEL JUGGLING

Chapter 5

When you really

want to get creative,

it's hard to ignore

the blending modes.

MASTERING THE BLENDING MODES

The blending modes are an integral part of the Photoshop experience. It's hard to imagine doing any creative Photoshop work without them. You could color correct an image, cut a silhouette, or do some other utilitarian task, but when you really want to get creative, it's hard to ignore the blending modes.

This chapter looks at blending modes from an experimental point of view. We will look at how to experience blending modes: where they are, what they let you accomplish, and how to combine them with other effects. We will also examine specific tasks and effects you can accomplish with them.

This chapter also looks at the math behind blending modes. Don't let that intimidate you, though. You don't need to be a mathematician, and there is no need to revisit your high school math days. The second part of this chapter proves no theorems and writes no algorithms; it takes more of a nuts-and-bolts view of how blending modes work.

This is a very important chapter, because while blending modes do indulge an action/reaction type of behavior (click this, see what happens), they are also the basis for most of the other filter options in Photoshop. This is especially true of the third-party filters, which continue to push the envelope. Having a solid understanding of blending modes will directly help your work with filters, which is tackled in the following chapter.

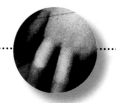

An Introduction to Blending Modes

The blending modes in Photoshop operate on the basis of comparison. Usually they compare the value of a pixel before and after an effect is applied, and they make a kind of value judgment. They determine if the final pixel value is lighter, darker, or a different color, or perhaps they add or subtract the value of both pixels. The result is that blending modes deliver results that would be almost impossible to achieve any other way.

For the sake of clarity, the existing pixel's value in the image is called the base value. The second pixel value, which is the result of the effect, is called the blending value. These values grow out of the following Photoshop scenarios.

Painting

When you use any of Photoshop's paint tools, The Normal blending mode changes the existing pixel value to the value of the current foreground color. In fact, the foreground completely replaces what is underneath, with no consideration of its value. When using any blending mode besides Normal, Photoshop uses the combination of foreground color and existing image pixel values to calculate the blending mode result. This is why you will see blending modes in the Tool Options palette for all of the paint tools. Click and hold on the blending modes pop-up menu, and select the desired mode before you begin (Figure 5.1). No blending modes are available for the Dodge/Burn tools, and a limited set of blending modes are available for the Sharpen/Blur tools. The Paint Bucket may also be used to fill in a pattern rather than the current foreground color, although either would be considered as the blend value.

Another anomaly in this example is the Rubber Stamp tool. As we've seen, the Rubber Stamp tool paints pixel values back in from various sources such as Snapshot or cloned portions of the same image. These source pixels act as the blend value, and the existing pix-

els become the base values. The values for the current foreground color do not come into play with the Rubber Stamp tool. Because of this, the Rubber Stamp tool operates more like a layering tool in the way it combines values.

Layers

Rather than use a brush to locally determine which pixel values are compared, layers take a more global approach. The blending mode for layers appears in the Layers Options palette (Figure 5.2). It considers the selected layer as the blend value and the layers beneath it as the base values. Layers allow you to create a cumulative effect, as multiple apply modes are applied to consecutive layers. Juggling variables in this kind of scenario can lead to unexpected and dramatic results.

Figure 5.1 *The blending modes from within the Paint Tools Options palette.*

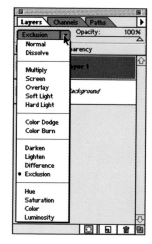

Figure 5.2 *The blending modes from within the Layers palette.*

Menu Driven Options

In addition to the changes you can make through brushes and layers, Photoshop allows you to use blending modes through menu-based commands as well. These commands are Fill and Stroke, which are located in the Edit menu, and Apply Image and Calculation, located in the Image menu. These modes are a hybrid of the other options looked at thus far.

The Fill and Stroke commands apply the foreground or background paint color to the existing pixel values, which allows similar blending effects as the paint tools. The Fill command goes a step further in that it allows you to fill with the contents of Pattern, Saved, or Snapshot, providing some of the same blending possibilities as the Rubber Stamp tool (Figure 5.3).

The Apply Image and Calculations commands go a step further in image combinations, while backing away from the foreground or background options. Apply Image allows you to combine a source image to a selected target layer. That source image could be the current image or another currently open image. Apply Image even allows you to specify an exact channel or layer within the source image (Figure 5.4). Once the source is specified, it is applied directly to the target layer, allowing some of the same blending options as the layers options.

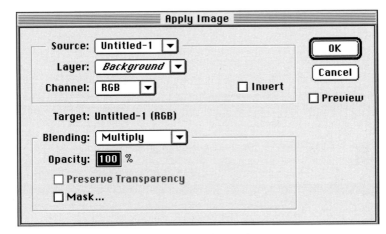

Figure 5.4 *The Apply Image dialog box showing the blend options.*

While Apply Image lets you combine two variables (the layer or channel from a source image) onto a selected target layer, the Calculations command allows an extra variable. Calculations allows the target to be any channel or layer within any open image rather than just a selected layer (Figure 5.5). While the blending options are applied in the same manner as Apply Image, Calculations gives a bit more control over the target.

Filters Options

Although Photoshop's native filters don't allow you to specify blending options from within the filter interface, you can blend the original and newly filtered pixels via the Fade command (Figure 5.6). In doing this, the new filter effect is the blend value, and the original image is the base value. Directly after applying a filter, select **Fade** from the

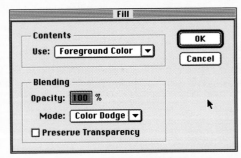

Figure 5.3 *The Fill (below) and Stroke (top) dialog boxes, showing the blending options.*

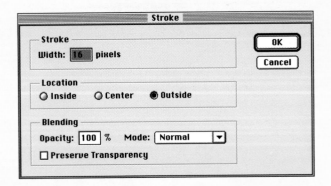

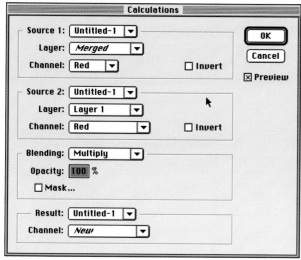

Figure 5.5 *Calculations allow more variable combinations, all of which can use the blending modes.*

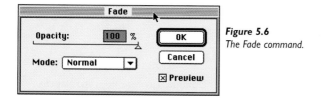

Figure 5.6
The Fade command.

If Photoshop allows you to alter a pixel, it will usually allow you to tweak that alteration with a blending mode. These blending options vary slightly in each location, so it's key to understand the basic differences of where they are accessed. In addition, the location determines exactly what values are compared, such as foreground paint values or Snapshot data. This understanding will also help you anticipate the blending mode options for each particular context.

Figure 5.7 *KPT Gradient Designer allows blending modes (called Glue Options) to be viewed before a filter is applied.*

Filter command, and experiment with how the pixel values interact. If you select any other command after applying the filter, the Fade option will be lost.

Many of the third-party filters do allow you to experiment with and apply filters directly from the filter interface. This can be easier than the two-step process of applying a filter and then going to the Fade command to see if a blending mode does what you expect it to. In addition to eliminating the two-step process, these third-party filters also allow you to see the blending results before you apply the filter (Figure 5.7). If the image is a large one or you have a slower CPU, this can be a real time-saver.

RECIPE: SOLARIZED MADONNA

Much of the power of Adjustment Layers lie in their ability to energize a single image without compositing or altering the image with filters. Adjustment Layers let you embellish and enhance certain areas or aspects of your image, while maintaining the freedom to make any changes along the way.

In this example, the source image is a relief sculpture from one of the facades of the Duomo in Florence (Figure 5.8). The subject matter and patina of the sculpture are compelling, but the overall variation and composition is a bit lacking. This image is useful as a departure point for developing an approach to Adjustment Layers.

1. Select the **New Adjustment Layer** command from the Layers palette menu, choosing the Curves option in the Type pop-up menu (Figure 5.9).
2. In the ensuing Curves dialog box, create an inverted

S-curve, by dragging the highlight handle from the bottom to the top, and the shadow handle from the top to the bottom. With the curve diagonal reversed, raise the left handle, and lower the right one, creating a backwards "S" shape (Figure 5.10).

Figure 5.10 Create an inverted S-curve.

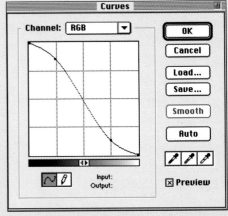

3. The resulting negative image is further enhanced by applying the Difference Apply mode to the Adjustment Layer. The Difference blending inverts lights and darks, while changing colors to their complimentary values. In this instance, the effect is tempered by reducing the Adjustment Layer's opacity to 44% (Figure 5.11).
4. Create a new Adjustment Layer, this time choosing the **Selective Color Options** from the Type pop-up menu. The red and cyan colors will be modified in an effort to get some of the red out of the image background and to fine tune the teal color.
5. Select **Reds** from the Colors pop-up menu, and set the sliders as follows: Cyan -31, Magenta 0, Yellow +68, Black -59. Leave the Method set to Relative, and make sure the Preview box is checked (Figure 5.12).

Solarized MADONNA sel color @ 25% (luminosity Curves, luminosity Curves Mask)

Figure 5.8
The original relief image.

New Adjustment Layer

Name: Curves

Type: Curves

Opacity: 100 % Mode: Normal

☐ Group With Previous Layer

OK

Cancel

Figure 5.9 The New Adjustment Layer dialog box.

Figure 5.11 *The Adjustment Layer result at 44%, with the Difference Apply mode.*

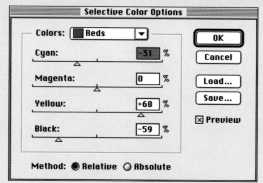

Figure 5.12 *The Selective Color Options settings for Red.*

6. Select **Cyans** from the Colors pop-up menu, and set the sliders as follows: Cyan -/+100, Magenta +56, Yellow -77, Black -0 (Figure 5.13). This takes much of the red out of the stone areas while making the blue in the shadows much richer (Figure 5.14).

7. Create a third Adjustment Layer derived from the initial Curves layer. With the Curves layer set as the target layer, (by clicking once on its name so it's highlighted), select **Duplicate Layer** from the Layers palette pop-up menu. Rename the layer Luminosity, and click **OK**.

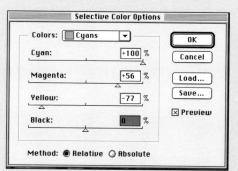

Figure 5.13
The Selective Color Options settings for Cyan.

Figure 5.14 *Combining the Curves and Selective Color Adjustment Layers.*

RECIPE: CONTINUED

8. When the layer appears, assign the Luminosity Apply mode, and turn off the Curves and Selective color layers. This shows the effect of the Luminosity Apply mode only (Figure 5.15).

9. These layers may be juggled and combined in various way to achieve a wide range of effects. The final effect shown here was created by arranging the layers from the top down as Selective Color, Curves, and Luminosity (Figure 5.16). The Opacity slider in the Luminosity layer was also reduced down to 88%, completing the effect.

Figure 5.16 The final image.

Solarized MADONNA sel color @ 25% (luminosity Curves, luminosity Curves Mask)

Figure 5.15 The results of the Luminosity Apply mode.

Basic Blending Effects

Blending modes offer a variety of options as they combine multiple images into a single composite. While there are many variations, the basic effects are to lighten, darken, change colors, or juggle the pixels in the image. Some effects vary depending on the blend values and can be hard to define. These effects are looked at later and are referred to as *chameleon effects.*

It is often easier to understand each blending option by the general effect it delivers, rather than be distracted by its specificity. The distinctions are intentionally broad, and the results can be hard to discern because the blend and base values are constantly in flux. Having said that, the following generalizations can help to clarify what the various blending modes can do. Understanding them in this way will allow you to employ a specific blending mode and have a good idea of what it will do to your image.

The base image is the Ole No Moire image from the Photoshop Calibration Sources folder (Figure 5.17). It is an excellent example, as it shows all of the main color combinations, along with a neutral gray area, flesh tones, and a graduated gray background. The blend image consists of an RGB gradient, an RGB/CMYK gradient, a 0-100% grayscale gradient, a black stripe, and a white stripe. These components are repeated twice over the base image, so that each component interacts with the base as much as possible (Figure 5.18).

Lighten Effects

The lighten effects are determined by whether the blending option results in a lighter result than the Normal effect. They tend to vary in terms of whether they lighten the entire tonal range, or just selected areas like the midtones or shadows.

SCREEN

Screen always lightens the image unless black is selected as the new value, in which case there is no change. In general, screen tends to wash out the entire image, applying an underexposed or bleached-out effect.

COLOR DODGE

Color Dodge effects vary substantially, depending on the blending value. The one constant is that pure colors in the base image remain pure, no matter what. This refers to any areas of pure cyan, magenta, red, blue, etc. As the blend values move towards tints, shades, and softer pastels, Color Dodge tends to let them dominate, as it hides the base pixels. Pure white, as a blend color, bleaches out everything in the base with the exception of the aforementioned pure colors.

LIGHTEN

Lighten always lightens the image. It looks at the base and blend values, and allows the lighter one to dominate every time. Darker blend values tend to drop out, letting the base show through. Light blend colors act like a mask, covering almost everything underneath.

Darken Effects

Darken effects are the obvious inverse of lighten effects. They apply an effect darker than the effect would be applied in the Normal mode.

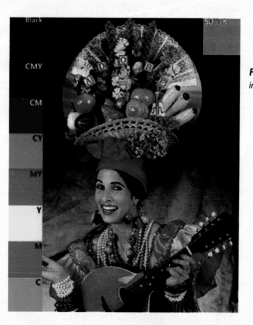

Figure 5.17 The base image.

Figure 5.18 The blend image shows all RGB, CMYK, grayscale, black values, and white values.

DARKEN

In the same way that Lighten always lightens the image, Darken always darkens it. Darken examines the two pixel values, and always selects the darkest value. The result is that dark blend values obscure what is underneath and light blend values leave the base untouched. Pure colors tend to tint the underlying image without obscuring it.

COLOR BURN

Color Burn will darken the image dramatically in almost every instance. Dark blend values dominate and obscure the base image, and white base values have no effect. It's interesting that when the blend values remain in grayscale, the blend effect is just a darkening or increase in saturation. If the blend value is more of a pure color, the blend effect is an intense saturation of the blend color onto the base image. Dark blend values dominate and pure colors oversaturate, which results in a very heavy dark effect.

MULTIPLY

Multiply is the inverse of Screen, in that it always darkens the image and that black blend values always dominate as they obliterate the underlying base image. Since Multiply always darkens, tonal values in the base image are sacrificed when the blend values reflect strong hues. The result is a strong color tint with flattened contrast in the base image.

Chameleon Effects

Chameleon effects impact the image differently, depending on the combination of blend and base values, and the context of the application. Although their results tend to vary, they are still somewhat predictable.

OVERLAY

Overlay can lighten or darken the image, depending on what color is being blended. As the blend value gets lighter or darker, so does the effect on the base. In the Multiply mode pure values in the base image remain constant in the Overlay mode. That means that black, white, and pure cyan, magenta, red, green, yellow, and blue, (and their com-binations), in the base values are untouched in the Overlay mode. This results in an effect that is applied in the 3/4 tones to the 1/4 tone range, either as higher contrast (if the blend value is grayscale) or as a color tint (if the blend value is a strong hue).

SOFT LIGHT

Soft Light will lighten an image in almost all cases, unless the blend values are very dark, in which case they darken it. Light blend values primarily effect the light areas in the base image; dark blend values effect the darker areas in the base image. Soft Light will softly apply the blend color to the base image. It will not obscure any of the base information; it will simply tint it with the hue or value of the blend pixel value.

HARD LIGHT

Hard Light will also lighten an image where the blend values are less than 50% black. The difference between Hard and Soft Light is that Hard Light has more of a bleaching effect, creating extreme darks and lights, pushing more contrast into the image. Black or white as a blend color will remain that way in the final effect, as it obliterates what is underneath. Conversely, a hue in the blend color will tint the underlying image, while still allowing it to show through.

Color Effects

Color Effects juggle the hue (color), saturation (intensity), and luminosity (tonality) of the comparative pixel values, resulting in image effects that can range from subtle to dramatic.

DIFFERENCE

Difference is the most glamorous blending effect, as it almost always delivers high-chroma, high-contrast results. Although Difference appears to be the least predictable blending mode, there is a method to its apparent madness. To begin with, Difference is built on the idea of inversion. Darks will change to light, and colors will assume opposite positions on the color wheel. That means that the image may invert to a negative. It also means that red may become cyan, yellow/orange become blue, and green become magenta. It gets tricky when you realize that these inversions only happen at certain times.

In general, pure color in the base image turns black, midtones are inverted, and lighter tones are either inverted or go black. A white blend value will invert the underlying base image all of the time, as it darkens whites and the pure base colors, inverting darker areas to a light color. Darker blending values have little effect on the lights and darks in the base image, while desaturating the purest base values to a light tint. The midrange values that remain are inverted.

EXCLUSION

Exclusion could be considered a kinder and gentler Difference mode. Applying a white blending value in Exclusion has exactly the same effect as it does in Difference, in that it reverses the base image, inverts the midtones, and changes pure colors to black.

It's when the blend values gets dark that the changes are evident. Dark blend values desaturate the base colors while maintaining light and dark values, although they do not reverse the midtone colors.

HUE

Hue is a very subtle effect in that it always maintains the luminance and saturation of the base color. Hue adds the hue of the blend color to the base image, while keeping the lights, darks, and saturation of what's underneath.

SATURATION

Saturation is another subtle color effect, since the tonal range and the hue of the base values remain intact and only the saturation is modified. If the blend value is black or white (no saturation), then the underlying base image is desaturated to grayscale. If the blend value is a saturated color, then the underlying base image is saturated more deeply, although there is no color or tonal change.

COLOR

Color applies the hue and saturation of the blend pixel with the tonality of the base pixel. The result is that the underlying image is tinted with the blend values. If the blend values are black, white, or grayscale (no saturation), then the underlying base image shows through as grayscale.

LUMINOSITY

Luminosity is the inverse of the Color mode, as the tonality of the blend pixel is combined with the hue and saturation of the base. The result is an image that retains most of the characteristics of the blend pixel, with subtle color tinting from the base values.

Pixel Modifiers

Pixel modifiers allow the blend and base values to react with each other selectively or in a way that disrupts their standard order. They tend to be more specialized and not always available in every instance.

DISSOLVE

The Dissolve effect only works when various degrees of opacity are present. If the blend pixel is at 100% opacity, it is applied at 100% to the image, obliterating the base image. When the blend pixel varies in opacity, then the underlying base image shows through via a rough stipple effect rather than a translucent blend. The base pixels become more visible as the opacity of the blend pixel is reduced.

BEHIND

Behind is only available when working in multiple layers, and then only from the Tool Options palette. In this mode, only the transparent pixels in a layer are modified. The visible pixels are unchanged. This is like the inverse of the Preserve Transparency option in the Layers Options palette.

CLEAR

Clear is only available with the Line, Paintbucket, Fill, and Stroke commands. For the Line and Paintbucket tools, it appears in the Blending modes pop-up menu in the Tool Options palette. For the Fill and Stroke menu commands, the Clear option shows up in the dialog box. Clear changes the base pixels to transparent, allowing the lower layers to show through.

RECIPE: CREATING AND USING ABSTRACT COLOR SELECTIONS

This recipe shows how to create dramatic abstractions for use in illustrations and fine art designs. Unlike filters and texture generators, this approach can deliver a level of precision and individuality that sets it apart from the crowd. The goal will be to create an interesting and colorful background abstraction as part of an illustration. The abstraction is created from a host of naturalistic images which maintain some of their realism even as they transition into the abstract.

You might not want to take this approach for every job, but when you're working on an image that needs extra attention, this approach can set the stage.

1. Begin by identifying source images that have a specific shape, texture, or color that you would like to incorporate in the final design (Figure 5.19). Some of the images will be used in their entirety, while others will feature a specific color range of the image.

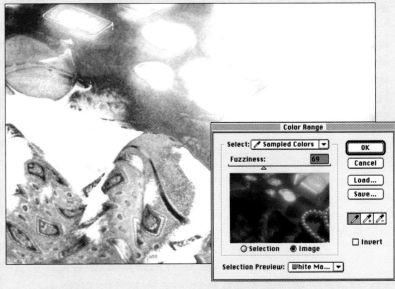

Figure 5.20 Using Color Range to sample the first source image.

Figure 5.19 The four source images.

2. To select a color range of an image, open it and choose **Select: Color Range**. With Sampled Colors active in the Select pop-up menu and White Matte selected in Selection Preview, click the eyedropper in the preview thumbnail to sample a color. In this case, the burgundy stripe in the scarf was selected, which also selected other colors similar to the one you have sampled throughout the image. The results of the sampling are reflected in the large image window as long as the White Matte option is selected. Adjust the Fuzziness slider until the active range of color creates a pattern or values that can be used in the design, and click **OK** (Figure 5.20).

3. Choose **Layer: New, Layer via copy (Command/Control-J)**. This copies the selected areas into a new layer.

4. Repeat steps 2 and 3 for any other source images that need it. In this case, the water highlights were selected from the second source image and copied or pasted into their own layer (Figure 5.21).

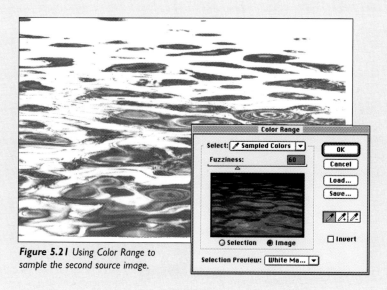

Figure 5.21 *Using Color Range to sample the second source image.*

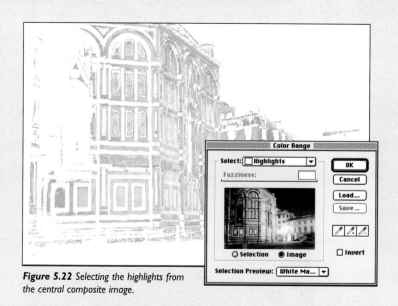

Figure 5.22 *Selecting the highlights from the central composite image.*

5. Open all of the source images and determine one image that will serve as the central composite image. With the Layers palette open and visible, click and drag the desired layer of each source image into the main image window of the central composite image. If you are using the entire image, drag the layer called Background into the central composite image. This will copy each source layer into the composite image as a separate layer.

6. To generate one last bit of source material, the background layer of the composite image is selected, and **Color Range** is selected from the Select menu. In this case, **Highlights** is selected in the Select pop-up menu, which automatically selects all of the light areas of the image (Figure 5.22). The resulting selection is copied and pasted into its own layer.

7. Select **Image: Rotate Canvas: 90 degrees CW** to rotate the entire canvas vertically.

8. At this point four layers are stacked above the background image in a vertical orientation. Hide all layers except for the background layer and Layer 2, and highlight Layer 2 as the active layer. Select the Difference blending mode in the Layers Blending modes pop-up menu (Figure 5.23).

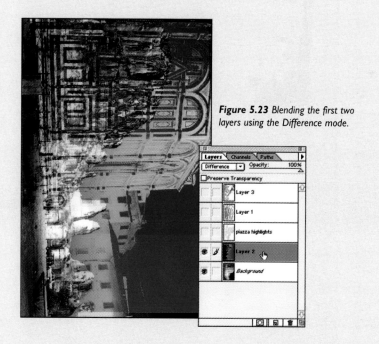

Figure 5.23 *Blending the first two layers using the Difference mode.*

RECIPE: CONTINUED

9. Erase most of the cathedral image over the sky by selecting a dark green color and painting out the cathedral in the background layer . The Difference mode shifts that particular green to the blue of the sky. (Figure 5.24).

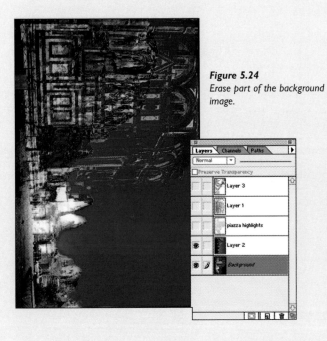

Figure 5.24
Erase part of the background image.

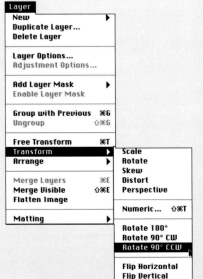

Figure 5.25
Select Rotate 90 CCW.

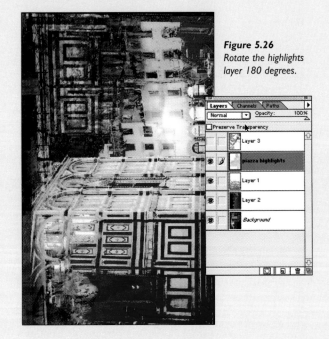

Figure 5.26
Rotate the highlights layer 180 degrees.

10. Highlight the waves layer and select **Layer: Transform: Rotate 90 degrees CCW** (Figure 5.25).
    Position the waves at the bottom of the image, and select **Color Burn** as a blending mode.

11. Activate the Piazza Highlights layer and select **Layer: Transform: Rotate 180 degrees** (Figure 5.26).

Figure 5.27
Apply a layer Mask

Figure 5.28
The final design.

12. With the Piazza Highlights layer still active, click the
Layer Mask icon at the bottom of the Layers palette.
With black and white as the foreground/background colors, double-click the gradient tool, set the Type to Radial
and gradient to foreground/background, and drag a gradient from the center of the highlight area (Figure 5.27).
This will mask the edges of the Piazza Highlight layer in a
circular fade (Figure 5.28).

13 Activate the top layer for added details to complete the
design (Figure 5.28). This design was ultimately repur-
posed to feature a specific object, and Layer 2 was dis-
abled to create another variation of the image (Figure
5.29).

Figure 5.29 *A variation on the
final design, eliminating one of
the layers and adding an object.*

BLENDING MODES

BLEND IMAGE	BASE IMAGE	RESULT

Screen

BLEND IMAGE	BASE IMAGE	RESULT

Color Dodge

BLEND IMAGE	BASE IMAGE	RESULT

Lighten

BLEND IMAGE	BASE IMAGE	RESULT

Darken

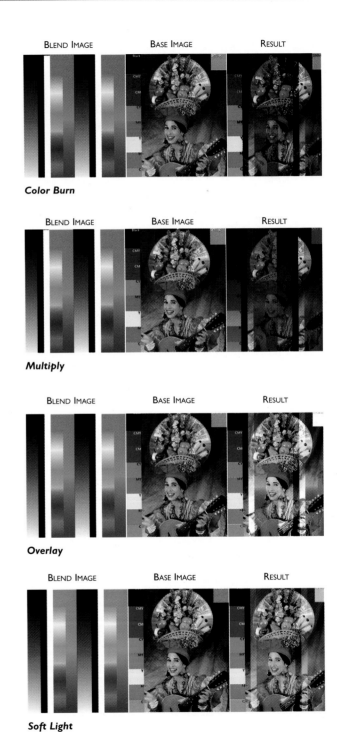

Color Burn

Multiply

Overlay

Soft Light

Hard Light

Saturation

Behind

Difference

Color

Exclusion

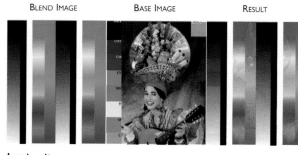

Luminosity

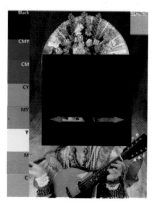

Clear

Hue

Dissolve

Blending Mode Strategies

While it's all well and good to look at what the blending modes do, it's even more important to have a sense of how to use them. In addition to using them experimentally, the following blending mode approaches can make certain tasks a bit easier.

Paintbrush Inversion Techniques

While it's possible to invert an entire image or selection by selecting **Image: Adjust: Invert**, there may be times in which you want to have the ability to invert an image at the tip of a paint tool. To do this, select any brush type, choose white as a foreground color, and select **Difference** as an apply mode. Painting into the image will invert the base pixels to a negative value, just as if you had selected **Invert** from the **Image: Adjust** menu (Figure 5.30).

This can be taken further by varying the opacity of the brush or by going back over areas already modified. Varying the opacity will result in a bright, multicolored abstraction that still follows the inverted base image to some degree.

Remember that the foreground color will be pushed into the shadows of the base image, which is why white makes the image look completely reversed. Selecting another foreground color, such as red or blue will force that color into the shadow areas (Figure 5.31).

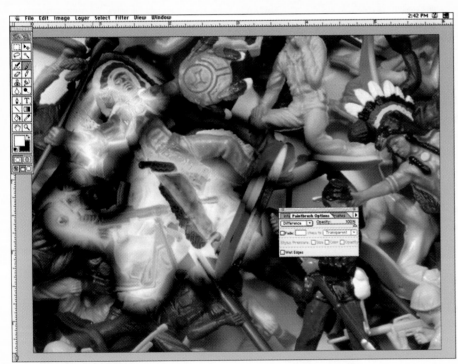

Figure 5.30 *Painting with white and the Difference blending mode puts image inversion at the tip of your brush.*

Figure 5.31 *The Difference blending mode pushes the selected foreground color into the shadow areas.*

Paintbrush Desaturation

In the same way that Difference inverts the base image as you paint, the Color blending mode desaturates the base image, while painting with white, inverting it to black and white. This can be very effective if you want to emphasize one area or object, while pushing everything else back to grayscale (Figure 5.32). It allows a more intuitive feel and selective application of the effect. To apply the effect, select any paint tool, select black or white as a foreground color, and choose **Color** as a blending mode.

Figure 5.33 *Using the Color blend mode to colorize a black-and-white photo.*

Figure 5.32 *Using white or black while in the Color blend mode desaturates the image as you paint.*

Paintbrush Colorize

The last paragraph looked at how to desaturate an image selectively to black and white using the Color blending mode. Another useful application of the Color mode is to selectively colorize areas of an image. As we saw in the last section, the Color mode leaves the tonality alone, changing only the color and saturation. This means that any selected color will be painted over the tonality of the base image, similar to the way you would hand color a black-and-white photo (Figure 5.33).

Another use for the Color blending mode is to select a color from the image itself, in order to paint a more solid area. Let's say you have an image that has a ground area that is primarily gray, but is speckled with other colors. Sample the gray color as the foreground and paint over the area. The other colors solidify to gray, making the area look more cohesive and less distracting. This can also be a very effective way to spot an image, removing specks of dust or other unwanted areas.

Increase Color Intensity

There are times when you want to give a certain area in an image just a little push. Perhaps it's the focal point, or maybe it's an area that's going flat as you convert to CMYK. A simple solution to this problem is to paint saturation into the image with a brush, via the Saturation blending mode. This will not change the tonality of the image at all, although the color may shift as saturation increases.

To apply the effect, select any paintbrush and choose **Saturation** as an Apply mode. The key to the application lies in what the foreground color is. If the color is desaturated, such as black or white, then the effect painted in will desaturate the base pixels. If the color is highly saturated, such as a bright blue, then the base image will become more saturated (Figure 5.34). A point that often confuses people is that the saturation changes to the base image still maintain the color and luminosity of the base. This means that any saturated blend color, whether it is blue or red or green, will have the exact same effect on the base pixels. This blending mode only looks at the saturation of the blend value, everything else comes from the base.

Using Opacity Variance

Remember to experiment with the Opacity slider as you are applying these various effects. In most cases, the opacity changes will simply temper the effect, making a Lighten effect a little less light, or maybe allow a bit of the lower base image to show through more. But in a few cases, the results can be unexpected.

When using Difference, this point is made in a most dramatic way. One way to illustrate this is to create a new layer over an image, and to fill that layer with white. Select **Difference** as a blending mode, set the Opacity slider at 100%, and view the results. As we saw earlier, the result is an inverted image. Leaving every other variable as it is, move the Opacity slider to

80%, then to 60%, 40%, and 20%. New images appear as the opacity is decreased. When using Difference, be sure to modify the Opacity slider to get a sense of the options available.

The Dissolve blend mode is also directly impacted by the Opacity slider. One way to visualize this is to add a simple mezzotint effect to an image. Create a new layer over an image, and fill it with a color using the Paintbucket. Set the blend mode on Dissolve, and move the opacity slider down to 80%. The top layer appears as a stipple pattern, giving the original image more of a graphic feel (Figure 5.35). The original image will probably suggest additional experimentation as well, such as different colors or screening two different images into a stippled composite.

As mentioned before, it's important to understand what Photoshop is doing as a blend mode is being applied. Without this understanding, you will get in the habit of blindly clicking through every blend mode until you see something you like. While there is nothing wrong

Figure 5.34 *It is possible to paint in higher color intensity with the Saturation blend mode.*

Figure 5.35 Using the Dissolve blend mode to add a graphic effect to an image.

with this every once in a while, it's kind of like a businessperson who opens a shop and just sits there waiting for the customers to come in.

Conclusion

A solid understanding of blend modes allows you to be more proactive with how you design, taking the blend modes into account as you make decisions. If you know that black will drop out of a certain mode, you may choose it to make a silhouette easier or to achieve a dramatic effect. This knowledge is like our businessperson gaining a knowledge of marketing and demographics to bring in customers.

You can do the same thing with the blend modes, only you're not reeling in customers, you're nailing down eye-catching effects, effects that set you apart as a Photoshop expert.

... the most important thing about filters is to know what they are capable of doing and how to harness their power.

FILTERS:
Beyond the Blend Modes

An Introduction to Filters

I originally wrote an elaborate description of how filters work and how they differ from blending modes. It featured an in-depth description of what a convolution kernel is and how various formulae can be inserted so that blurs, sharpens, and textures can be achieved. It looked at median averaging of pixel values along with other deeper secrets of how filters work.

Too deep perhaps? Well, I thought it was. I decided that the most important thing about filters is to know what they are capable of doing and how to harness their power. Beyond that, the other technical stuff is just indulging the curiosity of techies who might be reading this (and yes, I have just identified myself as their chief).

So it was with a twinge of techno-remorse that I abandoned this approach to the subject of filters and decided on a different approach. The problem for most designers is that there appear to be so many different types of filters out there. Photoshop has its set, but there are also the third-party possibilities like MetaTools, Alien Skin, and Andromeda, and others pop up all the time. The result is a vast array of products that claim to be so very that you must have them.

With that in mind, this chapter will look at some of the better packages, grouping options into similar bunches based on the final effects they deliver. Since this is a book on Photoshop, as opposed to a book on Photoshop filters, I will stick close to the filters that ship with Photoshop itself, mentioning third-party alternatives as the context warrants.

Basic Filter Types

Filters are calculations that apply a specific type of effect to an image or selection. Unlike the Blend modes that require two sets of pixel values to generate the final effects, filters can be applied to just one pixel value with more freedom and flexibility. (This is where the kernels and algorithm info comes in. I'm clinching my teeth and resisting the impulse).

In a general sense, a filter can apply a texture, create a distortion, modify an edge, or average a group of values (Figure 6.1). In a sense,

Figure 6.1 Filters can apply texture, modify an edge, distort, or average pixel values.

all filters texturize, surface map, average values, or modify edges. I list these categories to help clarify things. If they make sense to you then great; if not, then the information is still true, and you shouldn't get hung up on the groupings.

Texturizers

Texturizers emphasize the surface of an image, making it more noticeable. This becomes obvious when certain filters emulate the surface of physical objects such as paper or stone. That definition gets a bit confining though, as a texture can also be a repeatable pattern or digital abstraction.

The effects of a texturizer on an image are to unify it into a cohesive design. A texture effect can pull together a design where multiple images have been montaged into the same piece. This homogenizing effect can be especially effective if it is used to emphasize one object on the surface of the image (Figure 6.2). This can make the image seem like a photo or watercolor, with the object emphasized sitting on top of it.

Figure 6.2 Texture effects emphasize the surface of an image.

Other more pragmatic uses are in the design of Web pages and buttons. While textures do add additional file size to Web graphics, it is a trade-off many designers choose to live with. Even so, the images are still quite small and are excellent alternatives to large images that would be cumbersome to upload. Because textures can deliver a unique look, they have also been used extensively in presentation graphics, and their importance to the gaming industry is almost beyond mention.

TYPES OF TEXTURIZERS

Photoshop offers many texture options, especially in version 4, which incorporates the Adobe Gallery Effects filters into the main application. The Gallery Effects filters were a stand-alone series of plug-in filters that applied various artistic effects. Incorporated into Photoshop in the Filters menu under the submenus of Artistic, Brush Stroke, and Sketch, these effects apply a range of creative effects to your images.

Chalk on Paper Gallery Effects

Photoshop offers four basic ways of simulating chalk on paper: Colored Pencil and Rough Pastels are in the Artistic submenu, and Chalk & Charcoal and Conte Crayon are located in the Sketch submenu (Figures 6.3 through 6.6). Of these four, Colored Pencil offers the most image detail, sketching the image on a neutral gray background sheet. Rough Pastels predictably offers the least detail. Chalk & Charcoal is interesting in that its main color is determined by the current foreground color. Many Gallery Effects fil-

Figures 6.3–6.6 *The Colored Pencil , Rough Pastel, Chalk & Charcoal, and Conte Crayon filters (left to right).*

ters offer this option, which could be highly effective in the proper circumstance.

Conte Crayon and Rough Pastels allow you to control the actual surface that the effect is projected onto. This feature is also common to other Gallery Effects filters. A pop-up menu allows a choice from sandstone, burlap, canvas, or brick texture options. You also control the size of the texture relative to the image size, the light direction, and the degree of relief asserted by the texture. Since Conte Crayon gives control over the crayon color while giving a finer texture option than Rough Pastels, it tends to be used more frequently.

Crosshatch Gallery Effects

Crosshatch effects are differentiated from Chalk on Paper effects in that they tend to dramatically abstract the image, making little effort to hang on to detail. Located in the Brush Strokes submenu, the crosshatch effects filters are Angled Strokes, Crosshatch, Dark Strokes, and Ink Outlines (Figures 6.7 through 6.10). While their

Figures 6.7–6.10 *The Angled Strokes , Crosshatch, Dark Strokes, and Ink Outlines filters (left to right).*

names make them sound very different, they all appear to be basically the same filter. Dark Strokes produces more contrast. Angled Strokes is a bit rougher. Without labels, it would be very hard to distinguish one from the other.

Smudge Gallery Effects

When in doubt, Smudge! That must have been Adobe's motto when they created this type of filter option. These effects increase the contrast and either blur the edges, blunt the edges, or create a texture. These impressions usually don't quite convince, although you could place a few well-chosen effects in your bag of tricks.

Figures 6.11, 12 *The Cutout (left) and Poster Edges (right) filters.*

My favorite smudge effects filters tend to be those that offer the most variety and control, and that deliver effects that are more distinctive than a blotchy smudge. From the Artistic menu, they include Cutout and Poster Edges (Figures 6.11 and 6.12). These effects are sophisticated posterizing filters that allow for some very delicate graphic effects. They don't have that processed look that allows you to spot many effects right away.

Another smudge effect worth noting is the Accented Edges filter, located in the Brush Strokes submenu. While the dialog box doesn't look like much, it offers as wide a range of line width, lightness and darkness variation, and detail control as any Gallery Effects filter.

The smudge effects filters are numerous and can be repetitive. You can, however, achieve some great results with these filters—from the Palette Knife filter's distorting effect (Figure 6.13) to the Accented Edges filter's tight control and variation (Figure 6.14). Or, experiment with the Underpainting filter's fuzzy, textured effect (Figure 6.15).

Figure 6.13
The Palettes filter distorts color areas, creating a low-detailed effect.

Figure 6.14 *The Accented Edges filter.*

Figure 6.15 *The Underpainting filter gives fuzzy, textured effect.*

Pattern Gallery Effects

The pattern gallery offers a wide range of effects well worth exploring. The pattern effects are defined by their tendency to cover the image with a distinctive patterned texture. Is doesn't just sharpen or blur the underlying image, it does something more to the pixels.

A good example of this is the Plastic Wrap filter located in the Artistic submenu. Plastic wrap imposes thin highlights mostly into the shadow areas that resemble the folds of plastic storage wraps (Figure 6.16). There could be a number of good uses for this one, if you resist the temptation to overuse it.

Other pattern effects are Film Grain in the Artistic submenu and Spatter, which is in the Brush Strokes submenu (Figures 6.17, 18). These effects create a pattern of soft cells that soften the underlying image, almost seeping into it. Film Grain looks a lot like real film

Figure 6.16
The Plastic Wrap filter.

Figures 6.17, 18
The Film Grain (left) and Spatter (right) filters.

grain, in that it works to support the underlying image. Spatter does the opposite, breaking up the underlying image, similar to the way the Dissolve blend mode does.

Figures 6.19, 20 *The Reticulation (left) and Graphic Pen (right) filters.*

The last two pattern filters are similar enough to discuss together, although their effects are distinctive. They are the Reticulation and the Graphic Pen effects, both located in the Sketch submenu

(Figures 6.19, 20). Reticulation covers the image in a gray, pebbly texture that is somewhat soft and distorting. You wouldn't necessarily want to use this if image detail was important, although it does have a nice feel to it. It uses the foreground color to determine the effect, as does the Graphic Pen filter. Graphic Pen is a great filter in that it delivers convincing results, has a good amount of control, yet doesn't try to get too fancy. It really looks like a pen-and-ink technique.

Contrast Gallery Effects

Ironically, the following series of Gallery Effects filters that rely on contrast all seem to blend together. These effects reduce the image to some form of black-and-white graphic, with enough subtle variation to confuse, if not distinguish among them. I think the problem may be in the naming of the effects, because when you look at the results of these filters together, they are really quite impressive. The names just don't seem to stick with you.

The effects, which are located in the Sketch submenu, are Halftone, Photocopy, Stamp, and Torn Edges (Figures 6.21 through 6.24). The most basic effect is probably Stamp, which reduces the image to the foreground color and white, while softening the edges to emulate the crude offset process of a rubber stamp. It shows very little detail and has something of a processed look to it. Adobe softens the edges of Stamp, adds a bit more detail, and calls the result the Torn Edges filter. If you are applying this to a basic shape, in the right circumstances the effect could be quite believable. The Halftone filter is fairly successful in the way it puts down a patter of halftone dots as it

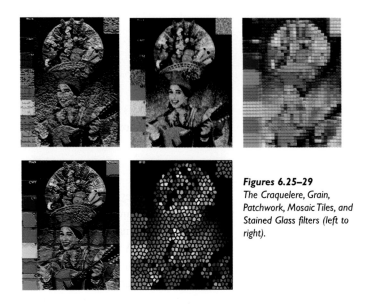

Figures 6.25–29
The Craquelere, Grain, Patchwork, Mosaic Tiles, and Stained Glass filters (left to right).

reduces the image to the foreground color and white. The Photocopy filter doesn't quite convince the viewer; it lacks the detail and specificity to make the results believable.

Gallery Effects Texture Filters

Maybe it seems funny to be so far into the section on texture before we get to this obvious inclusion. The reason, among other things, is that these options tend to be one-shot effects that are limited in their flexibility and scope. They are obviously textures, and if you need a brick wall or a sandstone texture, then you've come to the right place. But by and large, these filters are a bit harder to fit into your everyday workflow.

They are located in the Texture submenu and are Craquelere, Grain, Patchwork, Mosaic Tiles, Stained Glass, and Texturizer (Figures 6.25 through 6.29). Craquelere creates a surface of bumpy ridges over the image. Patchwork turns the image into a series of flat squares that roughly correspond to the tonality of the image. Mosaic Tiles imposes a grid of tiles with grout across the surface. While the effect is nice, I haven't found the right place to use it yet. Stained Glass is sort of a luminous mosaic tile, creating a grid of cells that roughly correspond to the image, with leading taking the place of grout.

Figures 6.21–24 *The Halftone, Photocopy, Stamp, and Torn Edges filters (left to right).*

The final effect, called Texturizer is more anonymous and therefore flexible, than the rest of the options in this section. It allows you to specify a texture pattern, such as canvas, burlap, sandstone, or brick; specify the light direction; and approximate size of the texture relative to the image. These controls are available in conjunction with other effects, but it's nice to have them separate as well. It is even possible to import your own texture into the mix, allowing more control over the final results.

The Remaining Gallery Effects Filters

The remaining effects are quite impressive, but they don't fit into any one category. Bas Relief, located in the Sketch submenu, is sort of like an anti-emboss (Figure 6.30). It actually digs the image out of a textured surface, creating an effect that is quite believable. A filter that abstracts a bit more than it should is the Chrome filter, also in the Sketch submenu (Figure 6.31). This filter obliterates the entire image, leaving a quivering mass of chromium soup in its wake. It would be nice if you could apply chromium effect while maintaining image detail, but the filter is resistant, and the results tend to be unrecognizable.

Figure 6.30 The Bas Relief filter.

Figure 6.31 The Chrome filter.

I've saved what I consider to be the best Gallery Effects filter for last, as we come to the Neon Glow filter (Figure 6.32). This unique filter, located in the Artistic submenu converts the entire image to just two colors. One color is taken from the foreground color, and is forced into the highlights. The other color is selectable from the filter interface and goes into the shadows (Figure 6.33). The filter gives full control over how much detail is in the image, as well as the balance between the two colors themselves.

Figure 6.32 The Neon Glow filter.

Figure 6.33 The Neon Glow interface.

The great thing about Neon Glow is the way that the colors interact. Some of the two-color interaction filters we've looked at so far have been clunky and lacking finesse. The Neon Glow filter makes up for any of the shortcomings of the others. The colors blend in soft transition that can be silky and seductive at one end of the spectrum and brightly evocative on the other. Take some time to familiarize yourself with this filter.

Third-Party Texturizers

If you are into textures, you really should run out and buy Kai's Power Tools and KPT Converter from MetaTools.

As mentioned earlier, the strength of Texturizer is that it gives control of the variables without limiting results. KPT Convolver takes all of the wraps off texture limitations, while keeping the package easy to use and navigate. You are given control over literally dozens of texture variables, all of which unfold and preview their results before your eyes, in real time (Figure 6.34). KPT Convolver is for those who are really serious about crafting their textures.

Kai's PowerTools is powerful in other ways. In addition to Gradient Design engines, Edge FX options, Spheroid generators, and loads of other fun effects, Kai's PowerTools also offers an extremely sophisticated Texture Explorer. Rather than having you delineate all of the variables, Texture Explorer does it for you, and you pick and choose what you like. You control the range of variation, size, and

application mode, but the texture itself is presented to you, as opposed to the crafting of a texture that takes place in KPT Convolver. The term explorer is well chosen in this respect.

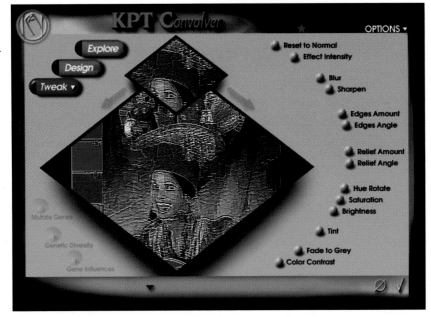

Figure 6.34 The KPT Convolver interface.

Distortion Filters

Distort filters stir up the pixels in an image, mixing them around according to a displacement map or lighting diagram. In some cases, the position of the pixels on the grid get mixed up, while at other times it is the tonality of the pixels that is modified. The result is that an image is warped, twisted, or colorized in reference to the overall frame of the image.

For example, the image grid might be twisted or stretched, or a series of light sources cast light across the surface. These modifications are made to the image in an external way, as the modifiers do not consider the value of the pixels in the actual calculations.

TYPES OF DISTORT FILTERS

An image can be distorted through grid changes or color changes. A grid change refers to taking an image and moving the pixels around in a predetermined pattern. In this instance, the pixel values do not change, but the position of each pixel does. These grid changes are notorious for taking a long time to process, so be careful if you want to twirl a 50MB image, especially if you're working on anything but a Power Mac or a Pentium. When we look at how distort filters modify color, we are primarily talking about how the Photoshop Lighting Effects filter works. This awesome filter applies a number of lighting modifications to the image, allowing a tremendous degree of control over all of the components.

Render Effects

The Render Effects filters are comprised of Clouds, Difference Clouds, Lens Flare, Lighting Effects, and Texture Fill (Figures 6.35 through 6.39). The Clouds filter replaces the image with a pattern of soft clouds, with sky and cloud colors that match the current foreground and background. Difference does the same thing using the Difference blending mode as it applies the two images. Difference is the more useful of the two effects, in that it maintains the original image. While you could always use the Fade command regardless of which Cloud option you used, Difference seems to integrate the effects into each other a bit better. In addition, you can still use the Fade command on the Difference Clouds options.

The Clouds options create interesting abstractions if you apply them repeatedly. This is most evident with the Difference Clouds

Figures 6.35–39 The Clouds, Difference Clouds, Lens Flare, Lighting Effects, and Texture Fill filters (left to right).

command, although interesting effects can also be achieved with the Clouds option. To see how this works, begin with a blank screen and select **Filter: Revert: Difference Clouds**. This should fill the screen with a cloud pattern. Repeat the Difference Clouds command with the keystroke **Command/Control F**, and watch as the pattern emerges. It can take several iterations for the image to evolve, but results should begin to appear after 10–20 applications. Initially, try this on a file that is fairly small, around 500KB–1MB, and the results should appear quickly.

The Lens Flare creates the impression of a sun flare on a camera lens. This is a nice effect with very believable details, especially some of the reflections on the inner lenses, which appear opposite the main flare.

Lighting Effects Lighting Effects is an interesting filter and very powerful, so much that it almost seems like a separate application or plug-in. There are so many buttons, sliders, and shapes at your disposal, and the preview is so responsive, that you just want to click, drag, and select every control.

Lighting Effects projects light onto your image, as if it were illuminated by an external light source. An example of this is the Billboard effect, in which the image looks like a billboard with lights shining down on it from the top. The lights almost always shine onto the surface of the image and usually tend to flatten the space.

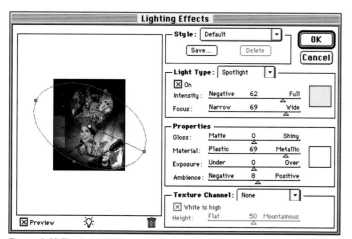

Figure 6.40 *The Lighting Effects interface.*

You bring up the Lighting Effects interface by selecting **Filter: Render: Lighting Effects** (Figure 6.40). The left side of the interface is a graphical representation of the effect, showing the image, the light sources used, and icons for creating and eliminating lights. As long as the preview button is checked, Lighting Effects shows you the results as you work. At the bottom of the left side is a lightbulb icon, which allows you to create additional light sources in the image. Lighting Effects allows 16 different light sources, each with its own individual properties, in a single effect. There is also the familiar trash can icon, so that you can drag a light to the trash if you don't want it anymore.

The lights themselves are very intricate in how they work. Each light consists of a center dot that represents the source itself, as well as a ring around the dot that is anchored by handles. You can click and drag the handles to control the radius of light projected by the source. Each light source can also be repositioned in the preview by dragging the center dot.

The right side of the interface is where all of the details come in. It can be somewhat intimidating to look at all of those sliders and try to make sense of what they do. Essentially, the right side asks you five questions:

- Do you want a preset style or shall we start from scratch?
- What kind of light do you have?
- What is the image being illuminated "made of?"
- What are the global lighting conditions the image exists in?
- Do you want to add any texture to the image?

The Style section addresses the preset question. It offers a pop-up menu that contains a host of preset options with all kinds of lighting configurations in various colors and styles. It also allows you to save and delete preset options to customize your own set.

The Light Type section tackles the question of what kind of light you have. The Light Type pop-up menu answers this in a broad sense, allowing you to choose from Omni, Directional, and Spotlight. Omni is like a bare bulb that radiates light in a circle; directional radiates light in one direction only, and spotlight casts a hotspot of light onto the image. There is a color swatch on the right that brings up a color picker to select the color of the light source. The Intensity slider

controls the strength of the light, and the Focus sets the path of the spotlights to a wide or narrow beam.

The first two sliders in the Properties section address the question of what your image is made of. The Gloss and Material sliders control how the light being cast is reflected by the image. The amount of light reflected back, along with the size of the highlight determines how we perceive the material an object is made of. Therefore, you can make it look as if the image is printed on a variety of substrates.

The second two Properties sliders look at the overall lighting conditions in the space shared by your image and the other light sources. The Ambiance slider determines whether the placed light source is the only light in the room or just one of many lights. This mainly controls the contrast and shadows in the effect. There is a color swatch in this section as well, which allows you to determine the color of the ambient light.

The Texture Channel obviously answers the last question: whether or not we want texture in the image. It applies a relief type of texture based on one of the existing channels, as specified by the Texture Channel pop-up menu. Interesting possibilities lie in our ability to create alternative channels to generate different kinds of texture patterns. The pop-up menu shows all of the existing channels in the image, so as long as a channel exists, it's available in the menu.

The wide range of controls in Lighting Effects is staggering, but with a bit of patience it's not too tough to wrap your arms around. With all those variables, there's no limit to what a creative person can come up with.

Distort Filters

Located in the Distort submenu of the Filters menu are 12 filters just waiting to bend, twist, and stretch your images. Of those filters, three are quite powerful and complex, eight are extremely similar in their operation and effect, and one seems strangely out of place. Earlier it was mentioned that distort filters apply global changes to an image based on a predetermined displacement grid. If you've been a little fuzzy on that concept, this set of filters should crystallize everything for you.

Simply put, the distort filters divide your image into a grid and then modify and distort that grid to achieve various effects. Let's consider the eight similar filters mentioned earlier, assuming there's some

Figures 6.41–48
The Glass, Ocean Ripple, Pinch, Polar Coordinates, Ripple, Spherize, Twirl, and ZigZag filters (left to right).

kind of strength in numbers. The eight similar distort filters are Glass, Ocean Ripple, Pinch, Polar Coordinates, Ripple, Spherize, Twirl, and ZigZag (Figures 6.41 through 6.48). Though not redundant, they perform basically the same function, using a different grid shape each time.

The Glass, Ocean Ripple, and Ripple look remarkably similar, to the point that it would be tough to differentiate their effects. These effects create distortion waves in the image that repeat over the surface. You have control over the size and frequency of the waves, and in some cases the density or focus. The remaining filters are the Pinch, Polar Coordinates, Spherize, Twirl, and ZigZag. These distort the image over a combination of axes, either running across the image in an X, or in some other pattern. A circle or sphere may be combined with the axis to create new patterns, as in the ZigZag and Spherize effects.

As one of the three powerful and complex Distort filters, the Wave filter is the central control center for wave generation effects. It allows you to specify the number of generators, which controls the overall direction complexity of the effect, the Min/Max Wavelength, and the image Amplitude (Figure 6.49). As the maximum wavelength goes higher, the wave effect gets longer and smoother. As it goes shorter, the waves are repeated with more frequency. The Amplitude controls the amount of distortion in the wave. This determines if the wave will be high and choppy, or low and smooth. The other controls in the window determine the shape of the wave patterns generated, the percentage of vertical or horizontal distortion, and a nifty Randomize button that creates random wave patterns.

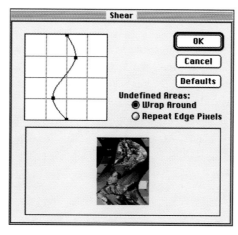

Figure 6.50
The Shear filter interface.

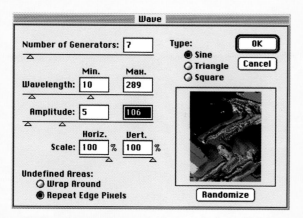

Figure 6.49 The Wave filter interface.

The Shear filter is the second complex and powerful Distort filter. Don't ignore this filter, assuming that it works like the Shear Control in Illustrator. The Illustrator Shear control is not necessarily problematic, it's just that I didn't have a use for the limited angled-sides effect that Illustrator's tool delivers. The first time I opened the Shear filter in Photoshop, my expectations were confirmed... or so I thought. There was a grid with a vertical line running through it with a handle on each end. Dragging the handle to one side or the other makes the image shear off to that side. As I was about to yawn and click **Cancel**, it struck me how much the grid in the Shear dialog resembles the Curves grid (Figure 6.50).

Sure enough, clicking in the center of the line created a handle that could be dragged to one side or the other, making a very complex wave design. Each handle and shape modification adds another level of complexity to the shear effect. It's the perfect effect for those who wish they could control a distortion to the last detail. The preview section at the bottom of the box updates the results quickly, and the whole experience of twisting and turning your image is really spellbinding.

The final Distort effect is the Displace filter. The Displace filter uses a second reference image as a guide in distorting the image. The second image must be a Photoshop image with a reasonable tonal range. Photoshop distorts the image by moving the pixels along a vertical and horizontal axis based on the values in the reference image. A neutral gray does not move the pixels at all, while a black value moves them the maximum negative direction, and a white value moves the maximum positive direction.

The first thing Photoshop asks for is the amount of horizontal and vertical offset, expressed in percentages. It also asks whether it should scale or tile the reference image, if it does not fit the main image, and how it should handle the pixels not affected by the filter.

I did say earlier that one of these filters was not like the others, and that distinction goes to the Diffuse Glow filter. Diffuse Glow lightens the image, making the highlight areas soft and misty. It looks like it should be in the Artistic set or maybe the Blur group. It's a nice effect, allowing basic control over the image graininess, glow amount, and the amount of clear area in the image (Figure 6.51).

Figure 6.51
The Diffuse Glow filter.

RECIPE: ADDING SMOKE & FOG

Sometimes a filter only gives you a starting point for adding effects to an image. For example, filters play a key role in adding a misty fog effect to this image, but they must be applied with an artist's hand. Remember that a filter does not perceive depth and perspective and works on all pixels globally or in reference to the pixels you select.

For this or any atmospheric effect, keep in mind that the mist grows thicker with distance, so you need to apply a thicker effect as the space recedes. That's one reason why you should be careful about what images you apply this to. If the image lacks perspective cues it might be hard to create a convincing illusion.

Since the success of this recipe relies on modifying edges and contrast, I've selected a black-and-white photo to work with. In addition, this image provides some excellent perspective markers that will work to our advantage (Figure 6.52).

Figure 6.53 Apply a Gaussian Blur with a pixel radius of 25.

Figure 6.54 Using curves to lighten the shadows

Figure 6.52 The original image.

1. Open the Layers palette, click on the lone background layer to highlight it, and select **Duplicate Layer** from the Layers palette pop-up menu.

2. With the duplicate layer active select **Filters: Blur: Gaussian Blur**, choose a pixel radius of 25, and click **OK** (Figure 6.53).

3. Select **Image: Adjust: Curves** and drag the 100% black point of the curve up to 70%, and click **OK** (Figure 6.54).

4. Click on the mask button at the bottom of the Layers palette to create a layer Mask for the active layer. With black and white selected as foreground and background colors respectively, select the Gradient tool and drag a linear gradient from the top section of the image, down towards the bottom (Figure 6.55). Since white reveals a mask and black conceals, the result will be a mask that hides the top section of the image, but allows the blurred layer to show through at the bottom (Figure 6.56).

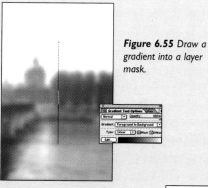

Figure 6.55 *Draw a gradient into a layer mask.*

Figure 6.56 *The result of the layer mask gradient.*

Figure 6.57
Create a new layer and fill it with a light cloud pattern.

is created, the thumbnail of the upper layer should indent slightly, indicating it shares the mask of the layer below. The result is that the cloud pattern is applied to the same lower image area as the blurred layer (Figure 6.58).

7. With the cloud layer still active, select **Filter: Distort: Shear**. Create random anchor points in the graph area and move them slightly from side to side in a subtle serpentine pattern. This will create a slight swirl effect to the mist. Be careful not to overdo this effect, or the image will not look natural (Figure 6.59).

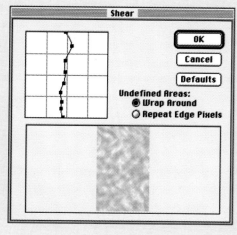

5. Create a new layer by selecting **New Layer** from the Layers palette pop-up menu. With white and a light gray selected as foreground and background colors, select **Filter: Render: Clouds**, filling the layer with a light gray cloud pattern (Figure 6.57).

6. Hold down the **Option** key and click in the Layers palette between the cloud and second layers. This will create a Clipping Group between the two layers, applying the mask of the lower layer to the upper one. The cursor should change to an icon of a pair of circles with an arrow before you click. After the group

8. It is important at this point to restate some of the dark areas in the fog area, to add more depth to the effect. Duplicate the bottom background layer and drag it to the top.

9. Click on the Layer Mask icon to add a layer mask to the duplicate layer. Choose black as the foreground color, select the entire image, and select **Edit: Fill**. This will fill the entire layer mask with black which hides the contents of the layer from view, allowing everything underneath to show. Be sure that the layer mask icon is active as you do this (it will have a heavy black box around it). If the image itself fills with black, then you had the Image icon selected. If that happens, undo the effect, select the Mask icon, and refill with black (Figure 6.60).

Figure 6.58
Create a Clipping Group with the clouds and blurred layer.

Figure 6.59
The Shear filter dialog box, adding some movement to the clouds layer.

Figure 6.60 *Fill the layer mask with black, hiding the contents.*

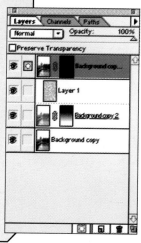

RECIPE: ——CONTINUED

10. Select the Airbrush tool, with a large brush selected. Choose white as a foreground color and paint into the layer mask, revealing the contents of the original base image (Figure 6.61). Vary the opacity and brush size to lightly restate the dark areas, maintaining smooth transitions (Figure 6.62).

11. Compact the image to one layer by selecting **Flatten Image** from the Layer options pop-up menu, and finish by tweaking the brightness and contrast. The variations here were created by selecting **Image: Adjust: Curves** and applying two "S" curves, alternatively emphasizing the lights or the shadows (Figures 6.63 and 6.64).

Figure 6.61 Airbrush the top image back into the layer mask.

Figure 6.63 Emphasize the darks to create a mist effect.

Figure 6.62 The results of painting the Layer Mask.

Figure 6.64 Emphasize the lights to create a fog effect.

Averaging Filters

Averaging filters modify a single pixel based on the values of the pixels around them. The result is an image that is more cohesive than it was before. An example that springs to mind are the Blur filters, which average the value of a single pixel with those around it, making it blend in with its neighbors.

TYPES OF AVERAGING FILTERS

The averaging filters in Photoshop are the Sharpen/Blur effects, Noise filters, and the Pixelate filters. With the exception of the Sharpen filters, averaging filters tend to remove detail in favor of applying a graphic style. This is certainly true of the Pixelate filters, and to some extent the Noise filters. An argument could be made that the Pixelate filters are actually modified versions of the Noise filters, tweaking the texture slightly to emulate various effects. Blur effects obviously reduce the detail in an image as well.

Because the Sharpen/Blur filters play such an crucial role in the imaging process, it is important to understand the nuances of the various filter effects. In making the transition from casual user to Photoshop expert, it is important to know when to use a Gaussian Blur as opposed to a Blur More. Keep that in mind as you go through this material.

Blur effects

As the last paragraph points out, it is important to understand when to use the Sharpen/Blur effects. The Blur effects get a great deal of use in smoothing transitions, de-emphasizing sections of an image, and re-establishing a focal point. All of the Blur filters are located in the Blur submenu, under the Filters menu.

The basic Blur options are the Blur and the Blur More filters. These options average the values of the pixels near the high-color contrast edges in the image. The averaging smoothes the areas between these transitions, making the entire image look softer. The Blur filter has a very subtle effect on the overall image, which is why the Blur More filter was added. The Blur More filter acts the same as the Blur filter, except that it is applied at 3 to 4 times the strength of the Blur.

Gaussian Blur is used the most. Selecting Gaussian Blur opens up a dialog box where you can move a slider that controls the amount of

blurring, along with a preview window showing the results (Figure 6.65). As long as the preview box is checked, the results will also be updated to the main image as well. Be patient if you are working this way though, as it can take a few seconds for the main image to catch up with you.

Figure 6.65 The Gaussian Blur dialog box.

Motion Blur blurs the image in one direction only, as specified by the directional wheel in the dialog box, or by typing a degree value. It is an enhanced version of the Wind filter found in the Stylize submenu, which would also be considered as a type of blur effect. The Radial blur is an interesting effect, underused primarily because it takes so long to apply. It takes so long, in fact, that it does not even offer a real preview of the image. Instead it simulates the effect with a series of gridlines. The Radial filter can either be a spiraling effect or a zooming effect, as specified by the radio buttons in the dialog box (Figure 6.66).

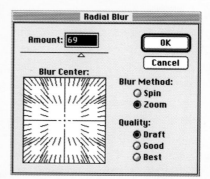

Figure 6.66 The Radial Blur dialog box.

The center of the blur or zoom can be moved by clicking and dragging within the preview box. The grid will move, although it can be hard to set an exact alignment since the image itself is not visible in the preview. You should also be careful about automatically selecting the Best mode, as opposed to the Draft or Good mode. The levels of quality may not differ that much from one setting to the next, although the time penalties between Draft and Best are significant (Figure 6.67).

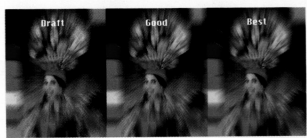

Figure 6.67 *The Draft, Good, and Best quality modes for the Radial Blur filter.*

The Radial Blur filter should be applied first on a low-resolution image. It's worth the wait if the effect is the one you want, but there is nothing more frustrating than waiting 15 minutes for an effect that is totally wrong. Definitely create a low-resolution version and get everything right before going to the final, time-consuming application.

The last and newest blur option is the Smart Blur, which Adobe introduced with Photoshop 4. Smart Blur combines the standard Blur options with an edge-sensitivity feature that delivers some very powerful results. Smart Blur allows you to blur certain areas in an image, while maintaining crisp edges in others. The overall effect is one of smoothing as much as blurring. Small specs of dust or distracting color can be removed, while keeping the primary edge contrasts in place.

The main controls for Smart Blur are Threshold and Radius sliders, which make this filter appear deceptively simple. There are also Quality and Mode pop-up menus to finish off the control options. It is important to remember that in Photoshop Threshold always creates a line of demarcation between two variables. It may be a selected or nonselected area, a point where a pixel is changed to either black or

white, or in this case, a point where an edge is blurred or not blurred. Moving the Threshold slider allows you to designate which edges are maintained and which are lost. That choice is determined by the value and contrast between the edge pixels.

Sharpen

The Sharpen filters are diametrically opposed to the Blur filters. The Blur filters break down the contrast between one area and another, while the Sharpen filters enhance the contrast. Located in the Sharpen submenu, the Sharpening options include Sharpen, Sharpen Edges, Sharpen More, and Unsharp Mask, although for most users there is Unsharp Mask and everything else. The reason is that Sharpen and Sharpen More affect every pixel selected; Sharpen Edges affects only the edge transitions in an image, and Unsharp Mask makes both edge and global modifications. Why go through three different dialogs, when you can control everything through the Unsharp Mask setting? That makes Unsharp Mask the main player in the Sharpening arena.

Unsharp mask offers three controls: Amount, Radius, and Threshold (Figure 6.68). If you've made it this far through this chapter, you probably have some idea of what those controls do. Keeping in mind that a Sharpen filter enhances the contrast between pixels, edges, and areas will make the various controls much easier to understand.

Amount refers to the degree of contrast added to adjacent pixels. Darker pixel values get darker, and lighter values get lighter as the image comes into focus. Radius considers exactly what value is to be sampled. Is it the value of a single pixel, 10 pixels, or maybe a broad

Figure 6.68 *The Unsharp Mask dialog box.*

area of 100 pixels? The more pixels selected, the more diffuse the effect will be, as the contrast value applied in Amount is spread over a wider area.

Threshold controls whether Photoshop looks at all the pixels in a selection or just at the edges. When Photoshop defines an edge, it uses the brightness values to do so. A variation in brightness values between adjacent pixels is what constitutes an edge. The key here is variation between pixels; Photoshop sees one pixel with a brightness of 100 and another with a brightness of 60, subtracts high from low, and determines a relative edge brightness of 40.

Since the Unsharp Mask Threshold default is set to 0, all pixels are affected in the image, regardless of how subtle their relative edge brightness may be. Move the Threshold variation up to 20, and only those edges with a relative edge brightness over 20 will be affected, while those below 20 will remain unchanged. What this means is that moving the Threshold controls to a higher setting can sharpen the higher contrast areas in the image, while keeping other softer areas from becoming too pixelated or fragmented.

Noise

The Noise filters do an averaging of a different sort. Rather than homogenizing the values of the pixels in a particular block, Noise simply adds random pixels to generate a coarse, grainy effect. In some cases, filters in the Noise area are intended to remove other specks and scratches that may already be present.

The Noise filters are especially valuable in creating cohesion without softening or blurring the detail. Adding noise can reduce banding in a graduated fill, for example, and in a pinch can reduce the pixelated "jaggies" in an image that has been interpolated up from a low resolution. These modifications come at the price of detail and sharpness, but are almost always better that having banded fills and jagged edges.

The Add Noise filter is the standard interface for adding noise. It allows you to control the degree of noise through the Amount slider, while allowing you to choose a distribution method of either Gaussian or Uniform. Uniform always delivers more of a smooth texture, while Gaussian creates a texture that is more coarse. The noise that is added consists of randomly generated colored dots, unless the Monochrome check box is selected, in which case the noise changes to grayscale.

Dust and Scratches is an interesting filter. It eliminates smaller, dissimilar pixels that are often the result of dust and scratches in a negative or transparency. The Radius slider allows you to specify how many adjacent pixels are averaged as the effect is calculated, and the Threshold slider determines which pixels are modified and which are ignored. It may take some experimentation to find a combination of settings that preserves the image, while getting rid of the image impurities, but in most cases it is possible. Remember, too, that if an image is resistant to a global application, the filter can be applied to selected areas in the image.

The final Noise filters are Despeckle and Median. Despeckle is a one-shot filter, in that it offers no dialog box and no controls. You simply select it from the Noise menu and it applies the effect straightaway. For this reason alone, many find it suspect. Despeckle ignores the edge transitions of an image, while blurring the remaining areas with the power of the Blur More filter. Median averages the colors in an image, which removes the impurities and specs that may be present. The only control for Median is the Radius slider, which determines the sampling area to be affected. Median creates a global blurring of the image, as it averages the color values.

Pixelate

An argument could be made for including the Pixelate filters in the Texturizer section of this chapter, rather than here in the Averaging section. While the Pixelate filters do generate a specific pattern, they do not reduce the image to the surface as much as the other Gallery Effects filters tend to. They place no emphasis on the substrate used, the light direction, or any other variables used by the Gallery Effects options. The result is the application of an overall effect that reduces the image to a graphic representation of what it once was, while staying away from any surface emphasis. Since this overall effect is applied based on the underlying pixel values, it's included in the Averaging section. As mentioned previously, these categories are not important except to divide all the effects into manageable sections, so don't get too hung up on the distinctions.

The Color Halftone filter applies a screened halftone effect to the image or selection. Unlike the Halftone Pattern filter, which applies the foreground and background colors in a two-color effect, the Color Halftone filter uses only CMYK values. It also allows you to specify

RECIPE: A HOLOGRAM EFFECT

This effect simulates the glowing iridescent holograms found on bank cards and collectibles. The act of converting the image to CMYK and printing it in a book will take away some of the edge in this effect, but it is still valuable, especially for Web and multimedia designs. This effect works best with objects against an open background, as in this tricycle (Figure 6.69).

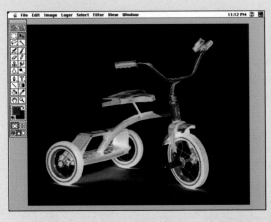

Figure 6.70
Invert the grayscale image.

Figure 6.69 The original image.

1. Select **Image: Adjust: Desaturate** to remove the image color while remaining in RGB.
2. Select **Image: Adjust: Invert** to reverse the image as a negative. This is important as the background must be dark for the effect to work (Figure 6.70).
3. Open the channels palette and select **New Channel** from the Channels Options palette. Select **Filter: Texture: Texturizer**, choosing **Canvas** as a texture, Scaling at 98%, Relief at 12, and Top as the Light Direction. Click **OK** to apply the effect.
4. Select **Filter: Blur: Motion Blur**. Set the angle at 0, and the Amount at 530, which sets the appropriate blur distance for an image of this resolution (Figure 6.71). Click **OK** to apply the effect. Note that this effect will be mediated by the pixel resolution. A pixel distance of 530 will give a different effect with a larger or smaller image.

5. Activate the Layers palette and select **New Layer** from the Layers Palette Options menu. Double-click the Gradient tool to activate the Gradient Tool Options palette and set the Type to Linear. Set the foreground/background colors to a bright red and bright green, and draw a diagonal gradient across the image (Figure 6.72).

Figure 6.71 Apply a Motion Blur to smooth the horizontal lines.

Figure 6.72 Draw a red-to-green gradient in the new layer.

6. Set the gradient layer Blending mode at Multiply to begin the glowing Hologram Effect (Figure 6.73).

7. Click on the background image layer to active it. Choose **Select: Load Selection** and choose the new layer #4 as the channel. You may get a message that no pixels are more than 50% selected. That's okay, as this is a subtle effect. You just won't see any flashing selection lines.

8. With the bright green still the background color, press **Delete** to create a light grid of green lines.

9. Choose **Select: Invert** to select the rest of the image. Select **Image: Adjust: Curves,** and raise the curve to lighten the image slightly. (Figure 6.74).

Figure 6.73 *Set the gradient layer Blending mode to Multiply.*

Figure 6.75
Apply a Gaussian Blur.

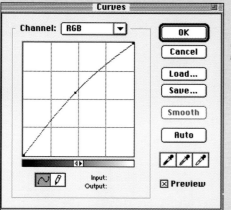

Figure 6.74 *Use Curves to lighten the image.*

10. Select **Filter: Blur: Gaussian Blur**. Choose a pixel radius of **3.6** and click **OK** (Figure 6.75).

11. Choose **Select: Invert** to reselect the thin gridlines. Click on the Marquee tool and click the up arrow on the keyboard three times to nudge the selection up by three pixels. Choose white as a background color and press **Delete** to finish the effect (Figure 6.76).

Figure 6.76 *The final effect.*

RECIPE: GREAT GRAYSCALE FILTER EFFECTS

When you want to convert an image to grayscale, the first tool you need to consider is Channels. Each channel appears as a grayscale version of the composite image with different emphasis on various tonal areas.

This recipe will push things further by combining the values of two channels to create a grayscale image that's better than any single-channel source. As an example of how to apply textures to single channels, the recipe shows how to create an intaglio etching effect in the same image.

It is commonly taught that you should look at the individual channels in a color image if you want to convert it to grayscale. The idea is that one channel will lend itself to grayscale better than the others, in terms of tonality and detail. To go a step further, try combining channels with the Calculations command.

1. Begin by examining each channel separately, looking for likely candidates to exploit. The red plate seems to have the best overall tonal range, but perhaps it's possible to do better (Figure 6.77).

2. To go further, we will blend two channels using Photoshop's Calculations command. Select **Image: Calculations** and choose different layers for the channels in Source 1 and Source 2. After looking at various combinations, I have chosen the red channel for both Source 1 and Source 2 (Figure 6.78).

3. Set the blending mode to **Multiply** and the Opacity at 75% to create a rich tonal range that goes beyond a standard channel selection (Figure 6.79). Select **New** as the result to save the channel as a separate file (Figure 6.80).

Figure 6.77 The image broken into RGB channels.

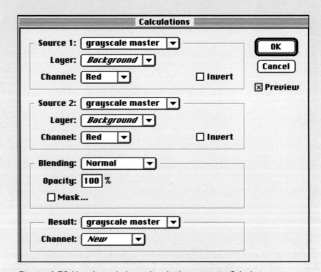

Figure 6.78 Use the red channel as both sources in Calculations.

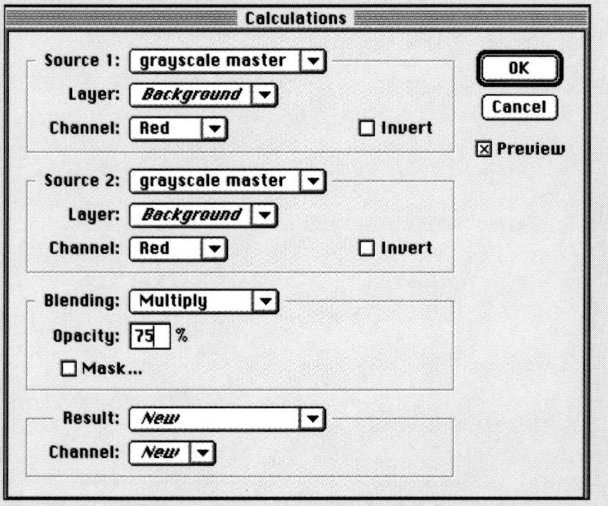

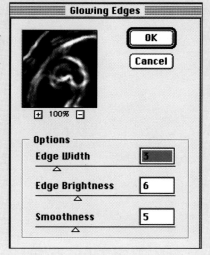

Figure 6.79 Use Multiply and 75% opacity to complete the grayscale image.

5. Highlight the blue channel and duplicate it as you did the red channel in step 4. Select **Filter: Noise: Add Noise**, and set the Amount at 64 and the Distribution to Uniform. Click **OK** to apply the effect (Figure 6.82).

Figure 6.81 Apply Glowing Edges to a copy of the red channel.

Figure 6.80 The final grayscale result.

4. To create an etching effect, highlight the red channel and select **Duplicate Channel** from the Channels palette pop-up menu. Highlight the new channel and select **Filter: Stylize: Glowing Edges**. Set the Edge Width to 3, the Edge Brightness to 6, and the Smoothness at 5. Click **OK** to apply the effect (Figure 6.81).

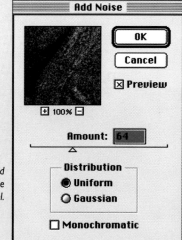

Figure 6.82 Apply Add Noise to a copy of the blue channel.

RECIPE: CONTINUED

6. Select **Image: Calculations**, and choose the altered red channel in Source 1, and the altered Blue channel in Source 2. Check the **Invert** box in Source 1, set the Blending mode to Multiply, and select **New** as a result. The final image looks like an intaglio etching (Figure 6.83).

7. Experiment with other Apply modes to fine-tune the effect further. By changing the Blending modes, you can really stretch the tonal range in the image. These variations were achieved with the Overlay (Figure 6.84), Soft Light (Figure 6.85), and Color Burn (Figure 6.86) modes.

Figure 6.83 *The final effect looks like an intaglio etching.*

Figure 6.84 *Using the Overlay blending mode.*

Figure 6.85 *Using the Soft Light blending mode.*

Figure 6.86 *Using the Color Burn blending mode.*

dot size and screen angles to be applied for each color screen, just as you would as you RIP an image to film.

Other interesting Pixelate effects are the Pointillize, Mosaic, and Facet filters (Figures 6.87 through 6.89). The Mosaic filter is a great one-step approach to reducing an image to the large digital squares that have come to represent digital imaging. Pointillize transforms the image to a series of larger dots that correspond to the underlying image. The result is a pointillist effect reminiscent of the French impressionistic painter Seurat, who reduced his images to small dots of color. Fragment offsets four separate transparent versions of the image on top of each other. The resulting grid offsets the image vertically and horizontally, giving the effect of double vision, or to be specific, quadruple vision.

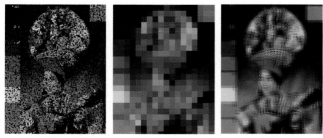

Figures 6.87–6.89 *The Pointillize, Mosaic, and Fragment filters (left to right).*

Crystallize, Mezzotint, and Facet deliver results that seem a bit redundant in the context of Photoshop's other filter effects (Figures 6.90 through 92). Crystallize creates a faceted effect that is just like the Stained Glass effect, only without the leaded borders between the cells. Mezzotint creates a dot or linear pattern that is better handled by the

Figures 6.90–6.92 *The Crystallize, Mezzotint, and Facet filters (left to right).*

Graphic Pen, Noise, Angled Strokes, and other Gallery Effects filters mentioned earlier. The Facet Filter is also reminiscent of the Dry Brush and Poster Edges filters found in the Artistic submenu. These three filters were significant in their day, but are being surpassed by the newer Gallery Effects filters.

Edge Filters

While we've looked at filters that consider the edges in an image in calculating a result, the filters in this section feature the edge predominantly as the final result. A sharpen effect may look at an edge in making the rest of the image look good, but for a Find Edges filter, the edge *is* the image. These effects apply a hard-edged graphic look to an image and usually sacrifice a great deal of detail in the process.

TYPES OF EDGE FILTERS

With the exception of the High Pass filter, which is located in the Custom menu, all of the edge filters are located in the Stylize menu. They are Emboss, Find Edges, Glowing Edges, and Trace Contour (Figures 6.93 through 6.96).

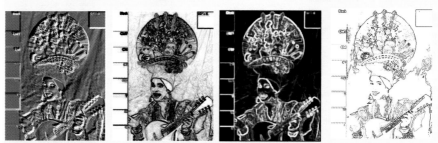

Figures 6.93–6.96 *The Emboss, Find Edges, Glowing Edges, and Trace Contour filters (left to right).*

The Emboss filter is the one that many Photoshop users learned first, because of its distinctive effect. Emboss works by finding the edges in the image, lining them with light and dark pixels, and reducing everything else to a neutral gray. The Emboss dialog offers a light direction wheel, which determines how Photoshop positions the light and dark pixels, simulating shadows and highlights.

RECIPE: — AN EMBOSS TECHNIQUE THAT REALLY WORKS

Lets face it, the Emboss filter applied right out of the box can be disappointing. It looks flat and only hints at an emboss effect. Furthermore, the way it handles color is so unnatural that it seems to put color where it's not wanted and avoids the areas where you do want color.

I've created this recipe to address these shortcomings and apply an emboss technique that looks more realistic. It involves applying the Emboss filter to each channel separately and varying the angles to achieve a realistic result. The initial image (Figure 6.97) is the same renaissance image we used previously in this chapter.

Figure 6.97 The original image.

1. Highlight the background layer and select **Duplicate Layer** from the Layers Palette Options menu.
2. With the new layer active, open the Channels palette and highlight only the red channel, while still viewing all channels. Select **Filter: Stylize: Emboss**, set the Amount to 200%, the Height at 6 pixels. And the Angle at -122. This will create a red offset in the image moving down and left (Figure 6.98).

Figure 6.98 Emboss the red channel.

3. Highlight the green channel while still viewing the composite image. Select **Filter: Stylize: Emboss**, set the Amount to 200%, the Height at 7 pixels, and the Angle at -90 (Figure 6.99).
4. As a variation, select the blue channel and select **Image: Adjust: Curves**. Invert the curve by dragging the lower-left black point handle to the upper-left, and the upper-right white point handle to the lower-right. The result is that the blue and green change places in the foreground and background of the final image (Figure 6.100).
5. One final variation is to double-click the background layer and save it as a normal layer. Drag it to the top and select color as a blending mode. This will color the emboss effect with the original colors from the image (Figure 6.101).

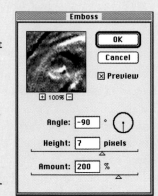

Figure 6.99 Emboss the green channel.

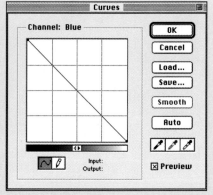

Figure 6.100 Invert the blue channel to swap the colors in the image.

Figure 6.101 The final image.

Find Edges, Glowing Edges, and Trace Contour are really three sides of the same coin. The filters all reduce the image down to the edges values and then process the values in some way.

The most basic approach is the Find Edges filter, a one-shot filter that replaces all of the nonedge areas with white, and the edges with black and multicolored strokes. Glowing edges replaces the nonedge areas with black, while widening and saturating the edge effect. It uses a dialog box that lets you control the width of the edge, its brightness, and the smoothness of how the edges interact. Glowing Edges can generate some very distinctive neon and glowing effects without much effort.

Trace Contour creates a light and wispy effect similar to a paint-by-number board before it's painted in. It basically takes the Find Edges effect and thins down the edge line by eliminating the black part, leaving the color. It features a Level slider with values from 0 to 255 that determines which edges are noticed and which are ignored. The higher numbers outlined are edges where light colors meet each other, while the low numbers accent edges where two dark colors come together. This one simple slider will generate a wide range of different images.

The last filter that focuses on edge effects is the High Pass filter, located in the Custom menu. The High Pass filter lowers the contrast in the entire image, except for the edge areas (Figure 6.102). The main difference between it and the find edge filters mentioned before is that the High Pass filter lets the edge effect fade into the gray, rather than create a hard line. It offers one slide that controls the radius of the effect. A higher radius will result in a light haze effect, and a low radius results in a gray image with dark lines delineating the image.

Figure 6.102 *The High Pass filter.*

Conclusion

This chapter only begins to touch on the filters options available in Photoshop. Once you've developed an understanding of what the various filters do, think about ways to combine them. In the same way that certain spices work well together when cooking, different filters can compliment each other. The areas of combination you should consider are in combining edge effects, color changes, and textural modifications. In many ways, the Gallery Effects filters are examples of these combinations, all rolled into one interface.

Also consider multiple applications of a filter. Why stop after one application? Some filters look great when applied 10, 50, or even 100 times. The Clouds and Difference Clouds filters are an example of this type of filter.

In general, filters are an area in Photoshop that will continually repay your efforts to explore and learn. The more you delve into the possibilities, the more you will discover.

p a r t

IMAGE COMPOSITING

3

Chapter 7

The answers lie

instead in the ability

to read and understand

the visual cues that

create the illusion of

space, depth, and

photographic reality.

COMPOSITING BASICS

Creating a Believable Composite

So far we've taken a hard look at Photoshop as an application—which buttons do what, how to open a menu, or how to apply a filter. While this logistical information is critical, it still doesn't answer the fundamental question of how to handle an image. I am referring to decisions such as how to colorize an image so that it still looks like a photograph, or how to choose images that will combine well in a composite. You won't find these answers in the Photoshop manual, or in most Photoshop books for that matter, because the answers have very little to do with Photoshop itself.

The answers lie instead in the ability to read and understand the visual cues that create the illusion of space, depth, and photographic reality. There have been many books written on this subject, and I won't pretend that this is the definitive text. It should, however, give you a good starting point, which combined with your visual intuition, will result in the ability to manipulate images.

Some Basic Assumptions

This chapter makes the basic assumption that we want to begin with a realistic image and modify it while maintaining a sense of realism. We could do this by adding other objects or figures, changing the time of day, or perhaps weaving two objects into each other, forming a hybrid. The fact is that if you understand the principles involved and are able to modify realistic images convincingly, you can do just about anything you desire.

Choosing Source Material

In working with realistic images, you should have a good selection of source material at your disposal. If you need to place materials into a scene and you only have a few images from which to choose, you may be backed into a corner and have to use inappropriate source images. With hundreds of images at your disposal, you have the luxury of choosing the perfect image, photographed at the right angle to meet your objectives. If you don't have the proper source material, you are at a tremendous disadvantage.

Another assumption is that you own the rights to the images you're using. It can be tempting to use images that you don't own, particularly when images can be easily grabbed off the Web or from a stock photo CD sampler. Don't do it.

Photograph the images yourself, buy the CD, or ask the appropriate permissions. It's the professional and ethical thing to do, and you will probably be saving yourself legal hassles.

One last assumption is a small but important one. It recognizes that the act of compositing is an art form all its own, and cannot be replaced by a 3D program or drafting application. 3D programs are terrific, but they lack a realistic look. The textures and light sources still appear artificial, and even the best of them look staged in comparison to a photograph. 3D imaging is great for a number of uses, but cannot take the place of compositing.

This chapter divides the basics of image compositing into three areas: perspective, focus, and color (Figures 7.1A and B). As you read through the chapter, think about selecting source materials that have consistency in these areas. Select an object photographed at the same camera angle as the room in which it will be placed, or perhaps maintain the same level of detail and focus. Keeping perspective, focus, and color in mind will help you create a realistic and impressive product.

Figures 7.1A and B The basics of image compositing are perspective, focus, and color.

160

The Importance of Perspective

I'm guessing that a fair number of readers went to art or design school. If so, you probably had to sit through at least one semester of perspective. If you think you know all there is to know, please bear with me, because I've got a hunch that it wasn't explained to you with digital imaging in mind.

Perspective translates the nuances of three-dimensional space onto the confines of a two-dimensional surface. As images are composited, the goal is to make sure that what is combined still follows those basic rules.

Types of Perspective

Perspective was one of the great discoveries of the early Renaissance, and the very foundation of most Western art until the twentieth century. It involved understanding how images foreshortened themselves as they receded from your eye. Images would recede toward a vanishing point that would sit on a horizon line somewhere in the distance (Figure 7.2). Things became more complex as multiple vanishing

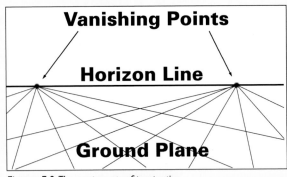

Figures 7.2 The components of perspective.

points were added, and two- and three-point perspective gave way to projection methods. This approach was known as linear perspective, and gradeschool kids have been using it to draw rudimentary cubes since Raphael was in diapers.

Figure 7.3 Atmospheric perspective causes objects far back in the landscape to fade.

As renaissance artists looked at how to create a convincing space, they noticed the way things got hazy as they receded in the distance. Those mountains in the background looked lighter and had a lot less detail than the hills in the foreground. This became known as atmospheric perspective and is critical in describing the far distance in panoramas and vistas (Figure 7.3).

We will consider atmospheric perspective as it relates to linear perspective, but understand that it also relates to focus and color. For that reason, atmospheric perspective will be discussed throughout the chapter.

Breaking Down the Components

Rather than plodding through the morass of vanishing points and angles, we can cut to the chase: If you watch your ground plane and horizon line, you're in pretty good shape. The ground plane reminds

Figure 7.4 *Objects improperly placed on the ground plane appear to be floating or sinking.*

Figure 7.5A and B *People are easier to composite due to their limited contact with the ground plane.*

us that we are bound by the laws of gravity, while the horizon line indicates that our eye maintains a fixed relationship to the horizon.

THE GROUND PLANE

Since we expect all naturalistic photos to follow the laws of gravity, it is important to anchor objects along the ground plane. While this may seem obvious, there are still areas in which to be careful. It is very easy to place the front of an object on the ground plane, while the rear is floating upward. It may be just one corner, or one side, but our eyes are sensitive enough to pick it up. And while it may be a subtle violation, it still translates into the vague notion that something is just not right with the composite. If you don't follow the angles of the ground plane, the object will either float off the ground in defiance of gravity or sink into the surface like quicksand (Figure 7.4).

Remember that the placed object plays a role in all of this too. Organic objects are more forgiving of errant angles than symmetrical angles. This means that it's easier to composite a person or a tree than it is a car or a brick wall. Gravity will demand that all four tires of the car be anchored to the ground. People and trees are organic, a fact which allows us to take certain liberties in compositing them into an image. As long as the feet or the trunk meet the ground, and the rest of the image follows the basic horizon requirements (see next section), we give the composite the benefit of the doubt.

People, poles, and other objects that occupy a narrow space are also easy to composite. This is because there is less surface meeting the ground plane (Figures 7.5A and B). The opposite extreme is a wall that recedes into space. The base of that wall has to hug the ground while maintaining symmetry and perspective. Don't try to composite walls unless your source imagery is perfect.

THE HORIZON LINE

Don't go crazy trying to envision an imaginary line stretching across the back of your image. Instead, think about where the camera was when the image was photographed. Was it looking down on the image, facing

Figures 7.6A–C *Examples of a high (right), median (below), and low (bottom) camera angle.*

Using Photoshop Tools to Modify Perspective

Up to this point in the chapter the emphasis has been on combining the proper images rather than manipulating pixels within Photoshop. This is because there is only so much that Photoshop can do without distorting an image beyond recognition. There are ways to nudge and tweak pixels, and a few instances where you can dramatically bend them to your will, but these efforts are secondary to choosing the right images.

THE TRANSFORM LAYER TOOLS

The Transform Layer tools take an entire layer and stretch and skew it back into the image. This type of distortion treats the layer as though it were printed on a piece of paper, tilting the image away from or towards you. The Transform tools do not respect the contents of the layer as they flatten and distort it. They see the layer as a grid, stretching the pixels accordingly (Figure 7.7).

There are many options in the Transform submenu, but the Distort option is the only useful feature for compositing. To activate

it, or looking up at it? What was the camera angle?

Looking down on an object creates a high horizon line. Directly facing an image from the side creates a median horizon, in which the ground plane levels off roughly in the center of the image. Looking up from beneath an object, such as underwater shots of the water's surface, create a low horizon line (Figures 7.6A–C).

To some degree, your source imagery will lean toward one of these angles. The question to ask yourself is, "Am I looking down at the ground, across a vista, or up in the sky?" The answer will directly impact the images you combine. As mentioned earlier, the objective is to anchor the object to a ground plane. For that reason, an object viewed from underneath is not going to fit into a birds-eye view very convincingly. Whether or not you want floating objects, the fact remains that you need to consider the camera angle as you combine source images.

Figure 7.7
The Transform commands distort the image grid in a global way.

Figure 7.8
*Using the **Transform: Distort** command.*

Figures 7.9A and B *The Transform: Distort command is an effective compositing tool for flat objects. Below, the painting is placed on the building and in the window.*

this option select **Image: Transform: Distort**. Photoshop draws a line around the layer with handles at the corners and the center. Each handle may be dragged independently of the others, creating various perspective angles (Figure 7.8).

Because of the dramatic and unnatural distortions applied by the Transform: Distort option, it doesn't have many uses. The one exception is when you want to make a flat image conform to a surface. Placing a flat sign on the side of a building, or a label on the side of a box, are two such examples (Figures 7.9A and B). If the image is supposed to be on a flat surface, then this method works very well.

Remember that the Transform options are applied only to separate layers, and will not work on the background layer. Copy the layer to be transformed to a separate layer and then apply the transformation. This allows you to reposition at will, using the Move tool, as well as the Transform: Scale and Transform: Rotate options. The Free Transform tool is not a good choice because it does not allow the corners of the image to be moved independently.

Command-clicking on the corner handles allows you to distort. Command-clicking on the side handles allows you to skew, and Control-clicking gives you a menu of options

A Focus on Focus

When we say that an image is in focus, we mean that it has crisp edges that are clearly defined. Conversely, an out-of-focus image has edges that are soft and blurry. Since we have all taken photographs with a camera, we are familiar with this definition. For the purposes of this section, however, I would like to broaden our understanding of focus.

Focus can also be considered as the presence of definition and detail—what a professional artist may call "information." A lack of focus can then be thought of as the absence of definition and detail, or information. This subtle difference allows us to consider things like clear and deliberate color or contrast as a focal point.

RECIPE: CREATING A FOCAL POINT

This exercise shows one method of imposing a focal point onto an image that lacks a compelling center. Color, sharpness, and perspective pointers are manipulated in the image to achieve the final result.

The original image is a scattered street scene, with no real focal point (Figure 7.12). The banners are the largest and most colorful objects, but they are scattered across the picture plane, and don't seem to be emphasizing anything in particular, except for the tassel that hovers over the man in the center. I decided to emphasize the man, while de-emphasizing the surroundings.

1. In the Layers palette, highlight the Background layer and select **Duplicate Layer** from the Layer Options menu. Select **Image: Adjust: Hue Saturation** and move the Saturation slider to -67, and the Lightness slider to +8 (Figure 7.13). Click **OK** to desaturate and lighten the copied layer.

Figure 7.14 The Diffuse Glow results.

2. Highlight the Background copy layer and duplicate it as in step 1. Drag the Background copy 2 layer to the top of the Layers palette, and select **Filter: Distort: Diffuse Glow**. Set the Graininess to 5, Glow amount to 14, and the Clear amount to 17. Click **OK** to apply a hazy diffusion to the layer (Figure 7.14).

Figure 7.12 The original image.

Figure 7.13 The Hue/Saturation settings.

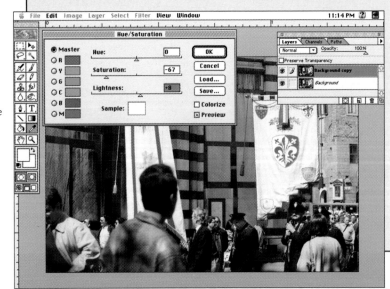

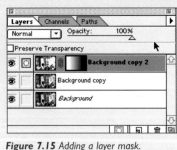

Figure 7.15 Adding a layer mask.

3. With the Background copy 2 layer still active, click the Layer Mask icon at the bottom of the Layers palette. Select the **Gradient** tool with white as the foreground, black as the background, and Linear from the Type pop-up menu. Draw a horizontal gradient from left to right, which puts the white part of the gradient on the left in the layer mask. The result is a diffuse effect that fades into the desaturated layer below (Figure 7.15).

4. In the Layers palette, click on the left thumbnail of the top layer to activate the image instead of the layer mask. Select **Filter: Blur: Gaussian Blur**. Set the Radius at 3.6 pixels, and click **OK** (Figure 7.16).

5. With the top layer (now Background copy) still active, select **Merge Down** from the Layers Palette Options menu to combine the top two layers. Select the eraser and choose **Airbrush** as an eraser type, and erase the top layer around the figure of the uniformed man in the center of the picture. Erase the tassel just over his head as well, allowing the brightly colored background layer to show through.

6. To make the tassel cord fade from saturated to desaturated, select the **Pen** tool and click once just above the tassel, and a second time at the top of the banner. Activate the Paths palette, which will show an active Work Path in its window. Double-click the **Eraser** tool, selecting **Airbrush, 100% Pressure**, creating a small brush that matches the diameter of the tassel cord. Click the **Fade** checkbox, setting the steps at 160. In the Paths palette, select **Stroke Subpath** from the options menu. The dialog reflects the last tool used, which will be the eraser. Click **OK** to stroke the subpath with the current parameters of the Eraser tool (Figure 7.17). The result is a straight eraser mark that follows the cord, fading out about half way up. The final image has a very compelling central point created by color, saturation, and sharpness (Figure 7.18).

Figure 7.16 *Applying a Gaussian Blur to the top layer.*

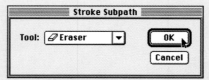

Figure 7.17 *Stroke the subpath with the Eraser tool.*

Figure 7.18 *The final image.*

RECIPE: — So You Want to Paint Like Rembrandt?

Rembrandt Van Rjin was a master at manipulating light and shadow in his paintings, controlling hard, soft, and lost edges to dictate compositional and optical focus. The paintings of this seventeenth-century Dutch Master provide valuable lessons for digital composition. (Figure 7.19).

This recipe shows how to make a photographic image take on the style and patina of a seventeenth-century Dutch portrait. Once the hurdle of creating believable brush strokes is overcome, the task of pushing and pulling at the lights and darks finishes things off. The original image (Figure 7.20) is one I found to be reminiscent of one of Rembrandt's self portraits.

Figure 7.19 Self Portrait by Rembrandt.

Figure 7.20 The original image.

1. In the Layers palette, click on the background layer to activate it, and select **Duplicate Layer** from the Layers Palette Options menu. Select **Image: Adjust: Curves** and modify the RGB composite curve to 255–191 and 0–88 (Figure 7.21). This will reduce the contrast in the new layer.

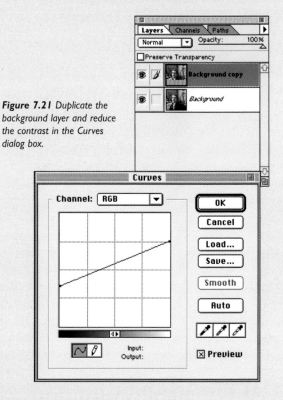

Figure 7.21 Duplicate the background layer and reduce the contrast in the Curves dialog box.

2. With black as the active foreground color, select **Filter: Pixellate: Mezzotint**. Choose **Medium dots** from the Type pop-up menu and click **OK** (Figure 7.22). This will cover the new layer with a layer of black noise.

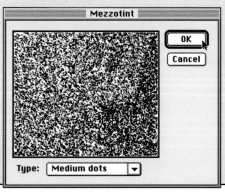

Figure 7.22 Apply the Mezzotint filter with the Medium dots setting.

3. Set the layer opacity of the new layer to 35% so that the background layer shows through. Select the **Smudge** tool and smear the dot pattern with short strokes, following the contours of the lower image (Figure 7.23).

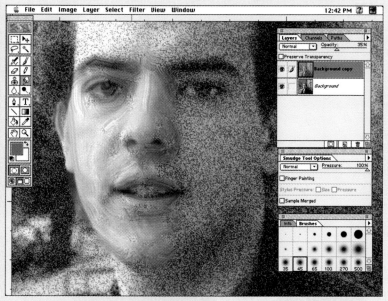

Figure 7.23 *Select the **Smudge** tool and smear the dot pattern to emulate brush strokes.*

4. I discovered an alternative design by selecting **Difference** as the layer blending mode and lowering the opacity to 55% (Figure 7.24). This isn't a Rembrandt, but it is a very nice image. I saved this to a separate file, and bumped the contrast to complete the design (Figure 7.25).

Figure 7.24 *Set the layer blending mode to Difference, and lower the opacity to 55%.*

Figure 7.25
The completed alternative design.

5. Returning to the Rembrandt design, activate the background layer and select **Duplicate Layer** to make a copy. Turn off the top two layers so that only the original figure image is visible, select the **Path** tool, and draw a path around the figure. In the Paths palette, double click the **work path** and save it as Path 1 (Figure 7.26).

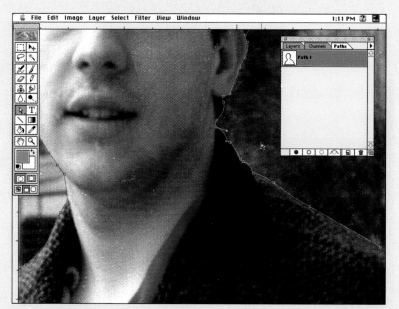

Figure 7.26 *Draw a path around the entire figure.*

RECIPE: ⎯ **CONTINUED**

6. Activate the background layer and select **Filter: Blur: Gaussian Blur**. Enter a radius of 61 pixels and click **OK** (Figure 7.27).

Figure 7.27 *Apply a Gaussian Blur to the background layer.*

7. With the background layer still active, select **Image: Adjust: Curves**. In the RGB composite curve, create input/output points at 67–20, 172–87, and 255–112. Select **Red** from the Channels pop-up menu and set an input output point at 121–164. Select **Green** from the Channels menu, and lower the input output point to 132–111. Select **Blue** from the Channels pop-up menu, and lower the input output point to 152–77. Click **OK** to apply the curve, which will create a warm red/sepia effect (Figure 7.28).

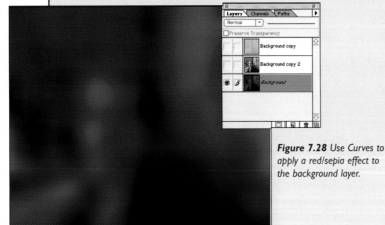

Figure 7.28 *Use Curves to apply a red/sepia effect to the background layer.*

8. Activate the Background copy 2 layer, which contains the original image. Open the Paths palette, activate Path 1, and choose **Make Selection** from the Paths Palette Options menu. Select a Feather radius of 1 pixel, make sure anti-aliased is checked, and click **OK** to create the selection. Choose **Select: Invert** and press **Delete** to delete the background layer (Figure 7.29). Finish the work on this layer by selecting **Multiply** as a blending mode, which allows the figure to pick up the coloring from the lower layer.

Figure 7.29 *Delete the background of the second layer, allowing the lower layer to show through.*

9. With the selection still active, select the top layer and choose **Filter: Blur: Gaussian Blur**. Set the Radius at 12 pixels and click **OK** (Figure 7.30).

Figure 7.30 *Blur the background with the Gaussian Blur filter.*

11. Choose **Flatten Image** from the Layers pop-up menu. Open the Paths palette and activate Path 1. Select **Make Selection** from the Paths Palette Options menu and choose **Select Invert** to reselect the background.

12. Select **Image: Adjust: Curves** and modify the RGB composite curve with input/output points of 64–21, 203–68. Select **Red** from the Channels pop-up menu and create an input/output point of 140: 94. Select **Green** from the Channels pop-up menu and create an input/output point of 64–79 and 147–193.

13. Complete the effect by burning the edges around the figure, and air-brushing specular highlights into the lips and nose (Figure 7.32).

10. Deselect the selection and select the **Toning** tool. Use the Burn Option tool to deepen the shadows in the image. Begin with a 10 to 15% exposure setting and gradually build the effect. Think about isolating the dark figure areas against light background areas, and blending the non-focal points into the shadows (Figure 7.31).

Figure 7.32 *The final image.*

Figure 7.31 *Use the Burn tool to deepen the shadows.*

Figures 7.10A and B *This image (above) comes alive by heightening the color and edge details (left).*

When choosing images to composite, consider whether the amount of detail between them is compatible. Is this image too soft to go in such a detailed setting? Is there too little contrast for the background? Fortunately, Photoshop allows us more control over these variables than it does over linear perspective, but they still should be considered.

An important point to remember is that focus is relative. An image that looks soft can sometimes be made to look sharper by blurring the background around it. Our eye is drawn to areas of contrast, whether it is sharpness, color saturation, or the tonal contrasts of light and dark.

If we've broadened the definition of focus, we have also broadened the definition of blurry. In the proper context, a desaturated gray background would be considered out of focus compared to a brightly colored subject (Figures 7.10A and B). Although it seems contradictory, this discussion of focus does adhere to our original premise of

striving for a realistic appearance. Carefully applied, these ideas can be effective and very convincing.

Consider the way the eye interprets information. Except for distant objects that are softened by atmospheric perspective, our eyes aren't able to handle out-of-focus objects very well. They converge on a subject, and the out-of-focus images create a double-vision effect. Figure 7.11 shows an example of this effect.

Figure 7.11 *Focus can also be expressed as convergence, creating a double-vision effect.*

What Focus Can Do

Visually, focus is a point in space. The material in front of and behind that space goes blurry. When creating a composite, think about the range of what is in focus—what photographers call depth of field. A deep depth of field tends to emphasize the entire scene, such as a landscape stretching into the distance. A shallow depth of field emphasizes an object in great detail, as the background fades to a blur.

As you are compositing, ask yourself if you are emphasizing an object, a corner of the room, or an open landscape. Decide what the focal point should be, and emphasize it with more detail. Then try to minimize the areas that might distract from the focal point.

Occasionally you can break the rules of focal point, and retain a realistic image. Our eye can only focus on one point in space at a time. An image could have two focal points and still be considered convincing. The work of Ansel Adams is the perfect example. His images bring everything into focus—everything from the distant mountains to the stream in the foreground.

Using Photoshop Tools to Manipulate Focus

Now that we understand the impact of focal points on an image, lets consider how Photoshop can make them happen. Photoshop will allow three types of sharpening and blurring: modifying an object, modifying an area globally, and modifying selectively with a brush.

SHARPENING OR BLURRING AN OBJECT

It is common to want to focus on an object while ignoring the area around it, creating the illusion of space and depth. The best way to achieve this effect is to select the object in such a way that the selection can be reactivated over and over again. In most instances this means drawing a path around the image, although a complex selection may require saving the selection to a channel. With the selection active, copy the object and paste it to a new layer or into the new image composite. At this point you have the following options:

- Apply any of the sharpen or blur filters.
- Use the Eraser tool in Airbrush mode, varying the opacity to soften the image as needed.
- Use the Sharpen or Blur tools. These apply very subtle effects in comparison to the filter options.
- Increase or decrease the contrast of the layer using any of the options in the Image: Apply submenu.

Think about the thickness of the object as it comes toward the camera. Are the edges as close to you as the center, or is the center closer, as it would be with a ball or sphere? You can often make a spherical image look sharper by softening the outer edges. If the object is flat, then a global treatment is fine. If it angles toward you, then the treatment should be a linear graduation like we will look at in the global area treatments.

If you intend to sharpen and blur the same object, it may be helpful to copy it to two layers, sharpening one, and blurring the other. You can then combine them by creating a layer mask for the top layer, or by just erasing it.

MODIFYING AN AREA GLOBALLY

Sometimes you want the focus in an image to move across an object, sharpening and blurring in a linear sort of blend. The effect is similar to the focus effects achieved by a 4x5 or 8x10 view camera. These cameras have a rear filmplane that pivots forward and backward, shifting the focus in the process. The best way to achieve this linear focus shift is to apply a Sharpen/Blend filter through a graduated layer mask. This approach allows the blur effect to fade into the layer below. It's hard to achieve this effect using a brush because it tends to get blotchy regardless of how careful you are.

MODIFYING SELECTIVELY WITH A BRUSH

There may be times when you want to soften an area rather than an object, and you don't want the mechanical feel of a linear focus shift. In this instance, you would copy the entire image to a second layer and apply the appropriate Sharpen/Blur filter. After applying a layer mask filed with black, you can paint the blurred area back in with an airbrush having selected white as a foreground color.

Even though they can be somewhat slow to apply, don't be afraid to modify an area with a large brush. Painting into a layer mask with a 200–500 pixel brush and a light opacity setting can deliver some smooth effects with a lot of control. The secret is to tap the area with short mouse clicks, rather than dragging with the mouse. Click and view the results, then click again, slowly building the effect. It may take a few seconds for the effect to materialize, but you have complete control and can undo if it's too much.

Getting the Color Right

Chapter 3 examined digital color, discussing how Photoshop turns numbers into colors. This section looks at how the color of light can integrate an object into a composite. The appearance of light shining on a object is crucial in creating a realistic composite. You can have

perfect perspective, focus, and detail, but if the color cast is wrong the whole thing falls apart (Figure 7.33).

Light Sources

Our eyes and brain are so good at averaging values that we usually don't even perceive light as having a color cast. It can be easier to see in photographs, but the fact remains that in real life and in photos, the color casts are there.

Interior light adds a yellow cast that shifts slightly to red in low-light situations. This is a result of incandescent lighting that is intended to create a softer effect. Remember too that interior light is very directional, because it's cast from an overhead light or desktop lamp. This lighting tends to cast strong shadows that are angled and directional.

When compositing objects into an interior scene, add yellow and red in various amounts, and consider whether it's necessary to lower the contrast. This is sometimes necessary because there is less light inside.

Interior florescent lighting is a stark green color that tends to lean slightly toward cyan (Figure 7.34).

Move outdoors, and the light turns blue. It also gets brighter with higher contrasts and tonal ranges. We know this because pictures taken outside don't need a flash, but take one inside and a flash is required. Outdoor lighting is also more uniform with less directional shadows, especially at mid-day when the sun is directly overhead.

Light changes in the morning and evening as the sun is rising and setting. The shadows get very directional and become softer as a result of low-light conditions. The color of the light also changes, shifting to a deeper red and yellow.

To some degree every image you work with is going to have one of these lighting characteristics. It is important to recognize them, and to get the best possible image. It's also important to recognize the color of shadows, matching their colors. It would be really easy if the shadows took on the same color casts as the highlights, but this is not the case.

Figure 7.33 *This dramatic example of light as color shows the impact light can have on an ordinary subject.*

Shadows tend to take on the inverse of the highlight color. This makes interior shadows run blue/cyan, fluorescent colors magenta, outdoor shadows red, and sunset shadows run purple and blue.

Since outdoor light is the brightest and most diffuse, the outdoor shadows are the most neutral. The light gets lower at sunset, so the blues and purples come out in the shadows (Figure 7.35). This is also

Figure 7.34 *The interior fluorescent lighting projects a green cast onto this street scene.*

Figure 7.35 *Sunset shadows shift toward blue/purple, as shown in the shadows in the clouds of this sunset.*

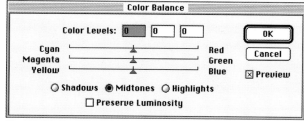

Figure 7.36 *The Color Balance controls.*

true in other situations where there is very little ambient light, or the lights themselves are low. The shadows cast by spotlights in a theater are a perfect example. Underexposed interior shots tend to show more color in the shadows as well.

Using Photoshop Tools to Change Color Cast

The best Photoshop tool for tweaking the color cast in an image is the Color Balance control. This command allows you to modify the color only in the highlights, mids, or shadows of an image, with color sliders providing numeric values. This tool allows for small shifts of color exactly where they're needed, as opposed to the larger shifts brought on by other Photoshop tools. (Figure 7.36).

Curves are also a good choice to adjust color or to create a stronger color shift. It's also possible to use the Variation controls to visually shift the color from one cast to another.

Conclusion

Keep perspective, focus, and color in mind as you choose images to composite. With carefully selected source materials, it's a simple matter of applying Photoshop's tools to achieve compositing effects that are convincing and professional.

Chapter 8

SPECIFIC COMPOSITING TASKS

Part of being an expert at something is being able to do the routine tasks better and more efficiently.

This book has taken an in-depth look at the complex and elaborate workings of Photoshop at the expense of standard production tasks. One could argue that anyone working in Photoshop should have a basic idea of how to clean up a hair in an image or cast a shadow from an object. Photoshop users perform these tasks routinely, so why should we spend time looking at how to do them?

The reason is that part of being an expert at something is being able to do the routine tasks better and more efficiently. Most Photoshop books assume that by telling you where all of the controls and commands are that you will figure this out for yourself. The reality is that most people try to do everything with just a few tools and commands. If the Color Balance command is good for minor color correction, it must be even better for changing an individual color in an image. Rather than using the Selective Color command (which is more appropriate in this case), they end up using the wrong tools for the job. Keep an open mind about different ways of performing tasks; it can make the basic tasks a lot easier, as well as opening up new options for some of the more creative stuff.

Dust & Scratches

If you do your own scanning, you eventually run into dust, scratches, or perhaps tiny hairs on the scanned image. This is especially a problem as you work at higher resolutions, which make blemishes and scratches more visible. If the blemishes are widespread, you should probably go back and re-scan. But if it's only one or two incidents, or perhaps if the negative itself is scratched, you may have no choice but to eliminate the spots digitally.

In traditional photography circles this is called *spotting*, in which finished photographs are painted with semi-transparent inks to fill in the various spots. The spots can include circular specks, short irregular hairs, or long straight scratches. It gets progressively harder to keep a natural look and to match the color as you go from specks to scratches. The essential elements in effective spotting are patience, high magnification, and solid rubber stamping skills.

The first step in effective spotting is taking your time. Double-click on the Magnifying Glass tool, which will automatically zoom the image up to 100%. Don't try to see blemishes at lower magnifications, as they have a tendency to hide, ultimately showing up when the job goes to print. Although your image may look great at 33%, always take the time to zoom to 100% and check for spots.

Once you are at 100%, drag the horizontal scroll bar all the way to the left, and the vertical bar to the top. This puts your view at the upper left corner of the image. Use the horizontal and vertical scroll bars to systematically move across your image, making sure it's clean.

The Rubber Stamp tool is the best choice to fill in the blanks because of its Clone-align feature. This allows you to set an source point (option-click) very close to the spot being painted, which makes color matching simple: Use a feathered brush that's just about the size of the blemish. If it's a hair or scratch, the brush should be as wide as the scratch. As much as possible, eliminate brushing back and forth to fill the area, since this can create brush strokes that look unnatural.

For long straight scratches, click the input point just above the scratch, sampling the area just above it as you paint. As objects intersect with the scratch, make sure that the input and paint points are positioned appropriately to maintain the proper relationship. This allows you to paint out the blemish in a single stroke without having to resample your alignment points as the scratch overlaps various backgrounds.

For larger spots where a small brush must be used, vary the opacity in the Rubber Stamp Options palette to feather and smooth the area. Begin lightly, and gradually build the effect, sampling from various areas in the image.

Creating Convincing Shadows

A critical part of compositing objects into a scene is the creation of believable shadows. Without a believable shadow, an object seems to be detached from its surroundings. Whether it's a thin black line of a shadow, or a sprawling cast shadow, a well handled shadow anchors an object and makes it part of the scene.

Digital technology has convinced a generation of artists that making a shadow is as simple as putting a dark to light gradation beneath an object. Digital shadows have always been flat and lifeless, lacking any color and nuance. Digital shadows do have their place in graphic and illustration application, but they are harder to craft for the photographic image. The end result is that most shadows are not very believable beyond an initial impression. This approach will show how to construct a believable shadow for the most detailed of images.

Once you've considered the color of the light source, the light direction, and the ground plane, (covered in the previous chapter) you need to actually construct the shadow and fill it in. To do this, follow the basic approach of creating a new layer, as follows.

- **Begin with a New Layer**. Start with a new layer on which to build the shadow. In addition to keeping the original image in pris-

tine condition, it also allows you to use various blending modes to help create the shadow. Assuming that you've composited an object into your scene, make sure that the composited object is the topmost layer, with the shadow layer next, and finally the original image as the background (Figure 8.1).

Figure 8.1 Create a shadow layer between the object and background.

- **Outline with Paths.** Use the Path tool to define the area for the cast shadow. This will allow a very repeatable outline that you can stroke and feather to varying degrees as needed. Remember that it's possible to stroke a path, and that the brush size and tool can be modified with multiple applications. This means that the Burn tool, the Blur tool, the Eraser, and the Smudge tool can all be used to modify the edge of a path (Figure 8.2). These tools are effective in shaping a shadow's edge, especially when combined with feathered brushes of varying sizes.

- **Feather the Edges.** As an alternative to stroking a path, you may wish to convert it to a selection and feather it. This is done by selecting **Make Selection** from the Paths Palette submenu, and then choosing **Select: Feather.** When painting a shadow into a

Figure 8.2 A shadow before (top) and after (bottom) stroking the path with the Eraser tool.

selection, remember that the edges in a real shadow will vary in relationship to the object casting the shadow. The closer a shadow is to the object casting it, the sharper its edges will be. As the shadow moves away from the object, its edges soften. To achieve this effect, convert the path to a selection many times, increasing or decreasing the feather as needed. Paint more of the shadow in with each feathered selection, gradually building the effect (Figure 8.3).

- **Use the Modify commands in the Select menu to grow or shrink the selection.** These commands can be used in tandem with the Feather command, shrinking and feathering the shadow selection as needed.

- **Create the Shadow.** How you paint the shadow effect depends a lot on the actual image. Because you want to keep the texture and surface characteristics of the ground plane, you should never apply a shadow with any of the paint tools. The Burn tool is a better choice, as is darkening or lowering the contrast with the Curves command.

- **Keep in mind that the shadow gets darker as it gets closer to the object** and as it is cast across a surface, away from the

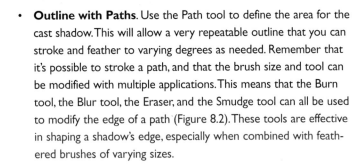

Figure 8.5 *The same shadow with red/magenta added, and slightly blurred.*

Figure 8.3 *Progressively softening a shadow's edges.*

Figure 8.4 *A shadow gets darker as it gets closer to the object.*

object, it lightens and diffuses. This goes hand-in-hand with the edge definition. As a shadow gets darker, its edges grow more defined (Figure 8.4).

- **A shadow is more than just darkening.** It can also involve blurring or softening the area within the shadow, as well as slight color changes (Figure 8.5). This is where isolating the shadow effect on a separate layer comes in very handy. Use the color controls such as Curves or Color Balance to add subtle color shifts to the shadows. Additive blending modes such as Multiply or Overlay can also work effectively, along with varying the opacity. By darkening, softening, and coloring the shadow area, believable results can be achieved.

Drawing in Photoshop

It's unfortunate that more people don't draw in Photoshop. I admit that the program has an overwhelming emphasis on image editing, and that certain features resist good mark-making. Having said that, some terrific effects can be achieved by indulging the act of drawing from within this imaging application.

Drawing as Mark-making

At its most basic level, drawing is mark-making. A properly drawn object can accent areas within an image, act as a transition between areas, or add an expressive effect (Figure 8.6). A carefully drawn object also signals the process of observation, showing that someone took the time to study and record the details of an object or scene. Regardless of whether or not these details register on a conscious level, they add impact to a drawing's presence.

Drawing within Photoshop

Figure 8.6 A good line drawing works as an effective counterpoint to a photographic image.

With all that a drawing obviously has to offer, why is it that more drawing capabilities are not evident in Photoshop? There are several reasons for this, many of which are due to the way Photoshop is designed and marketed as a product.

Photoshop has always been primarily a photographic application. It is marketed as a tool to replicate and modify the smooth soft-edged effects of a photograph. An obvious example is when Adobe began touting anti-aliasing as a key feature. The way anti-aliasing smoothes and fades the edges of a line or selection greatly enhances the overall photographic look of a montage. At the same time, it makes it really hard to draw. Much of the expressive quality of a mark or line is conveyed through its edges. A line's abrupt and subtle changes of direction carry a

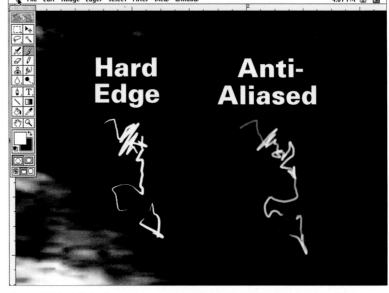

Figure 8.7 Anti-aliasing can remove the expressive characteristics of lines and marks.

great deal of meaning, and anti-aliasing blunts these characteristics (Figure 8.7).

The pre-layers versions of Photoshop made experimenting with drawing impractical due to the likelihood of losing what was underneath. While I will acknowledge that drawing and painting are secondary to Photoshop's treatment of photographic images, I will also defend the effects that they can generate. Positioned and executed properly, drawing and painting effects can add an effective counterpoint to Photoshop's imaging capabilities.

Drawing and Painting Options

Much of our efforts will be in putting gesture and emotion back into the drawing. The keys will be to work with anti-aliasing off, and to isolate as much area between separate layers as possible.

WORKING THROUGH LAYERS AND SELECTIONS

Working through various layers will allow you to isolate components of the drawing and to modify them more easily. The difference between working with an image and working with a drawing is that a drawing naturally suggests a layering process. A drawing communicates which line was drawn first, then second, third, and so on, based on what's on top and what's covered up. Segmenting a drawing between Photoshop layers allows a great deal of flexibility without detracting from the final look of the piece, or imposing unnatural restrictions to the process.

WORKING AROUND OBJECTS

One way to approach drawing in Photoshop is to accent a photographic image by drawing around it, obliterating the background. Done subtly, this can introduce a surrealistic effect, or simply serve to draw more attention to the object. A bolder treatment creates more of a graphic effect, while minimizing the processed look of the photograph. You can also achieve this effect by using the Behind blending mode from the Painting Tools Options palette.

If you lack drawing skills, it is possible to create a selection around the object itself before starting to draw. This will keep the image pristine and free from marks, as the drawing halos and highlights the object. An alternative to this approach would be to select and copy the object before drawing. Once the drawing is done you could paste it back down, or even restore sections using the Rubber Stamp tool using the Paint From Saved option. Other options would include pasting the object in its own layer and turning it on or off as needed. This option would also allow you to experiment with opacity variations, as well as with offsetting the top object layer from the outlines of the drawing below it.

WORKING WITHIN OBJECTS

The inverse of drawing around objects is drawing within them. This seems like a simple flip side of the first option, although there are subtle differences. The options, as far as working with layers, selections and opacity, operate in the same way, although the effects themselves achieve a different end. In drawing around an object, you either flatten or enhance the space the object sits in. This introduces a collage or graphic feel to the piece as a whole, at the same time that it shows reverence for the image. Drawing inside of an object de-emphasizes the image as a photograph, as it adds an emotional or expressive quality to the work (Figures 8.8A–C).

Morphing Effects

Today, morphing effects can be seen in many high-profile music videos and TV commercials. How can I make this object transform into that object? Whether it's a rock star or a charging tiger, the approach is the same. Video has the advantage of being able to complete the transformation before your eyes. Given that Photoshop is not an animation application, we must be content to show shots of an object undergoing a transformation.

To create a morphing effect in Photoshop is to effectively blend two images into a single object. This effect focuses many of the techniques discussed so far into a single objective, and is therefore a good ending point for this book.

Creating a Convincing Morph

When combining any two objects, there is a point at which the original image is no longer present, and the fixed image begins appearing. It's important to manage this transition as carefully as possible in terms of edges and textures, with the textural characteristics of one object giving way to the other. Remember that as we talk about texture, we are also talking about the reflective properties of the object as far as specular highlights are concerned.

It's also important to unify the object at the same time that we delineate differences in texture and contour. The unifying factors are the direction of shadows and the color of light. We are trying to convince people that the morphing object exists in a single place and time. That means that the shadows will all be cast in the same direction, and that the light will be consistent as far as interior, exterior, or artificial sources are concerned.

The recipe that follows pulls together many of the main points and procedures for creating morphing effects. The basic steps are to isolate the objects in separate layers, delete the backgrounds with paths, combine the object layers with layer masks, and modify color and texture as needed. Other options include using Distort filters to twist objects together, and using Blending modes to help combine the layers.

Figures 8.8A–C Starting with this renaissance relief image, drawing is applied inside and outside the central figure.

RECIPE: — MORPHING AN OBJECT

The initial image is the statuary figure from one of my previous designs (Figure 8.9).

Layer 8.11 The paint tube image.

1. Begin by selecting the **Magic Wand** and clicking inside the figure to begin a selection. Vary the tolerance and shift-click as much of the figure as possible. Click on the **Quick Mask** button and paint or erase the selection as needed (Figure 8.10). Use black and white to add and subtract from the selection.

2. Copy the selection and paste it back in, which automatically places it as a new layer called Layer 1.

3. Open the paint tube image (Figure 8.11) and select the **Move** tool. With the original image and the paint tube image both visible, drag the paint tube onto the original image. The window highlights slightly as you do so, as the paint tube image is copied into the original image.

Figure 8.9 The original image

Figure 8.10 Use the Quick Mask feature to fine-tune the selection.

Figure 8.12 Modify the paint tube layer with the Free Transform command.

4. The paint tube image comes in as Layer 2. Drag it below Layer 1, and select **Layer: Free Transform**. Rotate and scale the paint tube image, and line it up behind the figure in the top layer (Figure 8.12).

5. Hide Layer 1 and activate Layer 2. Because the background of the paint tube image is mostly white, you should use the Magic Wand tool to select it. Delete the background of this image, fine-tuning with the Eraser or Paintbrush as needed (Figure 8.13).

Figure 8.14 Apply an Unsharp Mask filter to the paint tube.

Figure 8.13 Silhouette the paint tube.

6. With Layer 2 still active, select **Filter: Sharpen: Unsharp Mask**. Move the Amount slider to 158%, with a pixel radius of 1.1 and a Threshold of 0 (Figure 8.14). Click **OK** to apply the effect.

7. Activate Layer 1 and click on the **Layer Mask** icon. With Black as the foreground color (which will conceal the layer as you paint), select the **Airbrush** tool and begin to lightly paint around the feet and lower legs of the figure (Figure 8.15). Vary the opacity of the airbrush in the Airbrush Options palette to create transparent and subtle transitions.

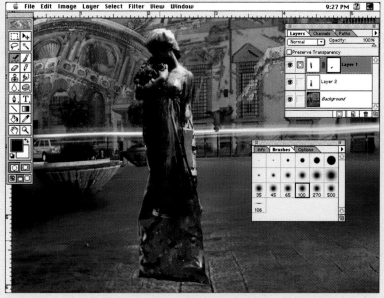

Figure 8.15 Conceal portions of the figure with a layer mask.

RECIPE: CONTINUED

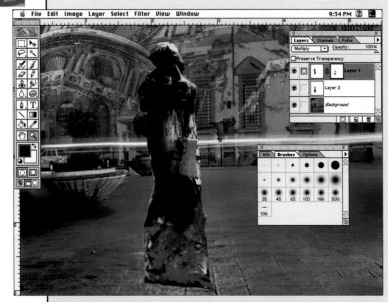

Figure 8.16 Apply a Multiply blending mode to the figure.

Figure 8.17 Paint in the edges and shadows of the price tag.

8. With Layer 1 still active, select **Multiply** from the Blending Modes Options in the Layers palette (Figure 8.16).

9. Select **Duplicate Layer** from the Layers Palette Options palette, creating a copy of Layer 1. Hold down the option key while selecting the **Layer Mask** icon, which conceals the image as the mask is created. With white as the foreground color, select the **Airbrush** tool and lightly brush in the face and shoulders of the figure, restating some of the highlights.

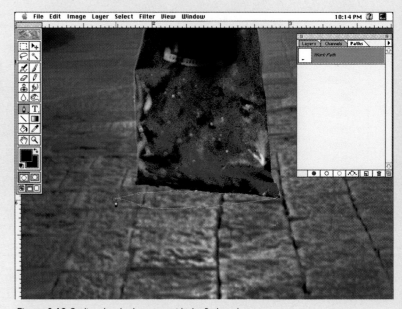

Figure 8.18 Outline the shadow area with the Path tool.

10. Select the Airbrush tool and zoom in on the orange price tag. **Option-click** to sample the colors of the tag and the shadows, and paint in the shadows, highlights, and hard edges (Figure 8.17).

11. Activate the Background as the active layer, and select the **Path** tool. Zoom to the bottom of the tube, and draw a path to outline

Figure 8.19 The Curves result for the shadow.

Figure 8.20 The final image.

the shadow cast by the tube figure (Figure 8.18). Select **Make Selection** from the Paths Palette Options menu and copy/paste the selection into a new layer.

12. Select **Image: Adjust: Curves** and adjust the Curves settings as follows: Cyan 161–99, Magenta: 175–112, Yellow 143–117, CMYK 91–0 and 182–50. The result is a dark, cool colored shadow (Figure 8.19).

13. The image is completed by adding a second paint tube. Steps 3, 4, 5, and 6 were followed in order to place, rotate, and silhouette the tube. Steps 11 and 12 were repeated to cast the second shadow (Figure 8.20).

Index

C

cache RAM, 6

Calculations command (Image menu), 110

Chalk & Charcoal filter, 132

chalk on paper gallery effects, 132

chameleon effects, 116

channels

    saving selections to, 43–44

    selections through, 36–37

Channels palette, 44, 100

Chrome filter, 135

Clear effect, 117, 123

clipboard, 10

Clipping Groups, 102–103

clipping paths, 30

Clone mode (Rubber Stamp tool), 15, 16

Clouds filter, 136, 137

CLUT (Color Look-Up Table), 63

CMYK color model, 54, 55, 64

color

    and compositing, 171–173

    correcting, 52–53

    curves, control with, 71–76

    and device variation, 51

    digitizing, effect of, 51

    duotones, using, 68–70

    intensity, increasing, 126

    inversion, 55

    and light source, 171–172

    manipulating, 66–67, 71–74

    and shadows, 172–173

    tweaking, 86

Color Balance control, 67, 173

Color Burn, 116, 122

Color Dodge effect, 115, 122

Color effects, 116–117, 123

Color Halftone filter, 145, 151

Color Look-Up Table (CLUT), 63

Color mode, 125

color models, 51

    CMYK, 64

    HSL (HSV, HSB), 65–66

    Indexed color, 63–64

    LAB color, 65

    reflective vs. luminous, 64

    RGB, 54–62

    secondary color spaces, 65–66

Color Picker, 65

Color Range command (Select menu), 32–33, 37, 118–119

color-based selections, 32–33

Colored Pencil filter, 132

Colorize check box, 19

ColorSync system, 51

compositing, 158–185

    blemishes, correcting, 177

    and color, 171–173

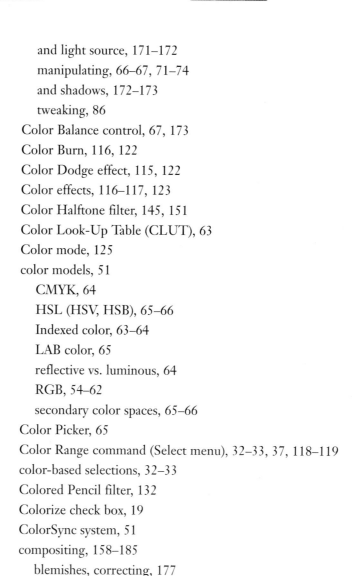